A Profit Manual for Attorneys

10 Things They Never Taught You In Law School

by Vincent Davis

COPYRIGHT AND DISCLAIMER

VINCENT DAVIS

Published by:
Leader Publishing Worldwide
19 Axford Bay
Port Moody, BC V3H 3R4
Tel: 1 888 294 9151
Fax: 1 877 575 9151
Website: www.noresults-nofee.com

ISBN-13: 978-1723446856
ISBN-10: 1723446858

DEDICATION

I would like to dedicate this book to my only son, Vinny, who lost his battle with drug addiction. Son, I may have never told you this but you, and your sister, were and are the loves of my life. I have taken many things we discussed and put into this book. I hope to make you proud.

CONTENTS

INTRODUCTION

This is the first page, but by opening this book you have already taken an important step towards increasing the success of your law firm. Congratulations in your quest to enhance your law firm and marketing skills

When I put pen to paper I found myself with an enormous amount of information I've developed over a 30 year career as an attorney, and with my own practice for 27 years. Many law firm marketing experts are NOT attorneys, and have never been an attorney. I, on the other hand, have been sitting across the desk from potential new clients (I'll call them PNCs throughout this book) for more than 30 years; and I've run my own law firm for the past 30 years. And as of this writing, my law firm is still running with 12 full time associates.

The strategies and techniques in this book have been developed over 30 years in the trenches, and literally with hundreds and hundreds of PNCs. The strategies in this book, when implemented with consistency and care, are guaranteed to make you more money with less effort. These strategies have helped law firms just like yours make hundreds of thousands of dollars – including your competitors.

This is the reason I have dedicated my life to law firm marketing and law firm consulting. Since starting my marketing company, I want to provide direction for small and medium law firms. I have been literally overwhelmed with the demand for marketing and law firm consulting.

As you follow the book and read the principles, remember it does not matter what type of practice area you are in. What matters is that you grasp the heart of the principles, the underlying lessons and strategies, that can help grow your law firm.

The best time to start is now, not tomorrow, not next week or next year.

Yours in success,

Vince Davis
Attorney at Law

P.S. If you would like to arrange a meeting to get a profitable third party perspective on your law firm law firm, please send an email to v@legalmarketingandsalescoach.com, and we will gladly point you in the right direction.

To learn how to avoid the three key mistakes all small and medium law firms make, visit www.legalmarketingandsalescoach.com.

1

Create a Powerful Offer

I'm not going to beat around the bush on this one:

Your offer is the granite foundation of your marketing campaign.

Get it right, and everything else will fall into place. Your headline will grab readers, your copy will sing, your ad layout will hardly matter, and you will have PNCs running to your door.

Get it wrong, and even the best looking, best-written campaign will sink like the Titanic.

A powerful offer is an irresistible offer. It's an offer that gets your audience frothing at the mouth and clamoring over each other all the way to your door. An offer that makes your readers pick up the phone and open their wallets.

Irresistible offers make your potential PNCs think, "I'd be crazy not to take him up on that," or "An offer like this doesn't come around very often." They instill a sense of emotion, of desire, and ultimately, urgency.

Make it easy for PNCs to purchase from you the first time, and spend your time keeping them coming back.

I'll say it again: **get it right, and everything else will fall into place.**

The Crux of Your Marketing Campaign

As you work your way through this program, you will find that nearly every chapter discusses the importance of a powerful offer as related to your marketing strategy or promotional campaign.

There's a reason for this. The powerful offer is more often than not the reason a PNC will open their wallets. It is how you generate leads, and then convert them into loyal PNCs. The more dramatic, unbelievable, and valuable the offer is the more dramatic and unbelievable the response will be.

Many companies spend thousands of dollars on impressive marketing campaigns in glossy magazines and big city newspapers. They send massive direct mail campaigns on a regular basis; yet don't receive an impressive or massive response rate.

These companies do not yet understand that simply providing information on their company and the benefits of their product is not enough to get PNCs to act. There is no reason to pick up the phone or visit the store, *right now*.

Your powerful, irresistible offer can:

- Increase leads
- Drive traffic to your website or law firm
- Move old product
- Convert leads into PNCs
- Build your PNC database

What Makes a Powerful Offer?

A powerful offer is one that makes the most people respond, and take action. It gets people running to spend money on your product or service.

Powerful offers nearly always have an element of *urgency* and of *scarcity*. They give your audience a reason to act immediately, instead of put it off until a later date.

Urgency relates to time. The offer is only available until a certain date, during a certain period of the day, or if you act within a few hours of seeing the ad. The PNC needs to act now to take advantage of the offer.

Scarcity related to quantity. There are only a certain number of PNCs who will be able to take advantage of the offer. There may be a limited number of spaces, a limited number of products, or simply a limited number of people the law firm will provide the offer to. Again, this requires that PNC acts immediately to reap the high value for low cost.

Powerful offers also:

Offer great value. PNCs perceive the offer as having great value – more than a single product on its own, or the product at its regular price. It is clear that the offer takes the reader's needs and wants into consideration.

Make sense to the reader. They are simple and easy to understand if read quickly. Avoid percentages – use half off or 2 for 1 instead of 50% off. There are no "catches" or requirements; no fine print.

Seem logical. The offer doesn't come out of thin air. There is a logical reason behind it – a holiday, end of season, anniversary celebration, or new product. People can get suspicious of offers that seem "too good to be true" and have no apparent purpose.

Provide a premium. The offer provides something extra to the PNC, like a free gift, or free product or service. They feel they are getting something extra for no extra cost. Premiums are perceived to have more value than discounts.

Remember that when your target market reads your offer, they will be asking the following questions:

1. What are you offering me?
2. What's in it for me?
3. What makes me sure I can believe you?
4. How much do I have to pay for it?

The Most Powerful Types of Offers

Decide what kind of offer will most effectively achieve your objectives. Are you trying to generate leads, convert PNCs, build a database, or increase sales?

Consider what type of offer will be of most value to your ideal PNCs – what offer will make them act quickly.

Free Offer

This type of offer asks PNCs to act immediately in exchange for something free. This is a good strategy to use to build a PNC database or mailing list. Offer a free consultation, free consumer report, or other item of low cost to you but of high perceived value.

You can also advertise the value of the item you are offering for free. For example, act now and you'll receive a free consultation, worth $75 dollars. This will dramatically increase your lead generation, and allow you to focus on conversion when the PNC comes through the door or picks up the phone.

The Value Added Offer

Add additional services or products that cost you very little, and combine them with other items to increase their attractiveness. This increases the perception of value in the PNC's mind, which will justify increasing the price of a product or service without incurring extra hard costs to your law firm.

Package Offer

Package your products or services together in a logical way to increase the perceived value as a whole. Discount the value of the package by a small margin, and position it as a "start-up kit" or "special package." By packaging goods of mixed values, you will be able to close more high-value sales. For example, including a free hard copy book with every service purchased.

Premium Offer

Offer a bonus product or service with the purchase of another. This strategy will serve your bottom line much better than discounting. This includes 2 for 1 offers, offers that include free gifts, an in-office credit with purchases over a specific dollar amount. For example, as an attorney, you might offer $$ off your regular retainer fee, or $$ off the PNC's bill or an extra service, like offering to review minute orders and/or outline strategy, etc.

Urgency Offer

As I mentioned above, offers that include an element of urgency enjoy a better response rate, as there is a reason for your PNCs to act immediately. Give the offer a deadline or limit the number of spots available.

Guarantee Offer

Offer to take the risk of making a retainer purchase out of the equation for consideration by your PNCs. Guarantee the performance or results of your product or service, and offer to compensate the PNC with their money back if they are not satisfied. This will help overcome any fear or reservations about your product, and make it more likely for your leads to become PNCs.

Create Your Powerful Offer

1. Pick a single product or service.

Focus on only one product or service – or one product or service *type* – at a time. This will keep your offer clear, simple, and easy to understand. This can be an area of your law firm you wish to grow, or old product that you need to move off the shelves.

2. Decide what you want your PNCs to do.

What are you looking to achieve from your offer? If it is to generate more leads, then you'll need your PNC to contact you. Do you want them to visit your website? Sign up for your newsletter? How long do they have to act? Be clear about your call to action, and state it clearly in your offer.

3. Dream up the biggest, best offer.

First, think of the biggest, best things you could offer your PNCs – regardless of cost and ability. Don't limit yourself to a single type of offer, combine several types of offers to increase value. Offer a premium, plus a guarantee, with a package offer. Then take a look at what you've created, and make the necessary changes so it is realistic.

4. Run the numbers.

Finally, make sure the offer will leave you with some profit – or at least allow you to break even. You don't want to publish an outrageous offer that will generate a tremendous number of leads, but leave you broke. Remember that each PNC has an acquisition cost, as well as a lifetime value. The amount of their first purchase may allow you to break even, but the amount of their subsequent purchases may make you a lovely profit.

2

Increase Sales Immediately with Scripts

What do playbooks, prompts, guides and scripts all have in common?

They are all popular tools that dictate or guide human behavior toward a desired outcome.

Playbooks help coaches tell sports teams specifically how to play the game to overcome an opponent. Prompts help to kick-start writers and other creative professionals when stuck in a rut. Guides provide a series of instructions so that a person or team of people can complete or implement a specific task. Film scripts tell actors how to act for a particular part.

If you're in the business of acquiring new PNCs, you also know about sales scripts. Sales scripts are tools that guide your case managers during interactions or conversations with potential PNCs.

A large number of law firms use scripts, either as a way of maintaining consistency amongst a team, training new staff, or enhancing their communication skills. They may have a single script, or several, and may change their scripts regularly, or use the same one for years.

What most law firms overlook, however, is that the script is a living, breathing, changing member of their team. They may be internal documents, but they deserve just as much time and effort as your marketing collateral.

Do You Really Need a Script?

The short answer is yes. You absolutely need a script for any and every PNC interaction you and your team may find yourselves in.

Sure, countless law firm owners work every day without a script. If you own your own law firm, chances are you're already pretty good at communicating with potential new clients (PNC's). But, if you are not using scripts, you're only working at half of your true potential – or half of your potential earnings.

Scripts don't have to be "cheesy" or read verbatim. They act as a map for your process, and provide prompts to trigger your memory and keep you on track. How many times have you made a call to a PNC that didn't work out the way you wanted it to? Scripts dramatically improve the effectiveness and efficiency of your case and case management processes.

A comprehensive set of scripts will also keep a level of consistency amongst your staff and the PNC services they provide.

Once scripts are written, memorized, and rehearsed, they become like film scripts; the reception staff or case managers can breathe their own life and personality into the conversation, while staying focused on the call's objectives.

Why Your Scripts Aren't Working

If you are currently using scripts in your law firm, are they working? Are they as effective as they could possibly be? How do you know? When was the last time they were reviewed or updated?

Scripts are like any other element of your marketing campaign – they need to be tested and measured for results, and changed based on what is or is not working.

Measure the success of your script based on your conversion rates. Of all the people you speak to and use the script, how many are being converted from leads to actual paying PNCs?

When evaluating your existing scripts, ask yourself the

following questions:

How old is this script? What was it written for? Scripts are living, breathing members of your firm. They need to be written and rewritten and rewritten again as the needs of your PNCs change, your product or services change, or as new strategies are implemented.

Does this script address all the PNC objections we regularly hear? Every time you hear a PNC raise an objection that is not included on the script, add it. The power of your script lies in the ability to anticipate PNC concerns, and answer them before they're raised.

Does this script sound the same as the others? Your scripts are part of the package that represents you as a law firm. There should be a consistent feel or approach throughout your scripts that your PNCs will recognize and feel confident dealing with.

Is everyone using the script? Who on your staff regularly uses these scripts? Just the reception staff? Only the top performing case manager? Make sure everyone is singing from the same song sheet – your PNCs will appreciate the consistency.

Types of Scripts

Depending on the product or service you offer and the marketing strategies you have chosen, there are countless types of scripts you could potentially prepare,

When you sit down to create your scripts, it would be wise to start by making a list of all the instances you interact with your existing or potential PNCs. Then, prioritize the list from most to least important, and start writing from the top.

Here are some commonly used scripts, and their purposes:

Sales presentation script

Each time you our your staff conducts a consultation or in some fashion communicates with a PNC, they should be using the same or a slightly modified version of the same script. This script will include sample icebreakers, a presentation on benefits and features of the product or service, and a list of possible objections and responses. These scripts should also help alleviate some of the nervousness or anxiety associated with speaking to a PNC and/or their family.

Closing script

Closing scripts help you do just that: close. This could include a list of closing prompts or statements to get the transaction started.

This type of script also includes a list of possible PNC objections, and planned responses.

Incoming phone call script

Everyone who calls your law firm should be treated the same way; consistent information should be gathered and provided to the PNC. The person answering the phone should state the company name, department name, and their own name in the initial greeting. This goes for both the main line, and each individual or department extension.

Direct mail follow-up script

Scripts for outgoing calls that are intended to follow up on a direct mail piece are essential for every direct mail campaign. They are designed to call qualified leads that have already received information and an offer, and convert them into PNCs. These scripts should focus on enticing PNC's to act, and on overcoming any objections that may have prevented them from acting sooner.

Market research script

Scripts that are used primarily for the purpose of gathering information should be designed to get the PNC talking. A focus on open-ended questions and relationship building statements will help to relax the PNC, and encourage honest dialogue.

Difficult PNC script

Just as every reception staff or case manager needs to practice the case and hand-off process, you and your staff also need to practice your ability to handle difficult PNCs. If you operate a law firm, this is especially important, as difficult PNCs often present themselves in front of other PNCs. These scripts should help you diffuse the situation, calm the PNC down, and then handle their objections.

Creating Scripts

Creating powerful scripts is not a complicated exercise, but it will take some time to complete. Focus on the most vital scripts for your law firm first, and engage the assistance of your reception staff and case managers in drafting or reviewing the scripts.

Your Script Binder

Keep master copies of all of your scripts in one organized place. An effective way to do this is to create a binder, and use tabs to separate each type of script.

You will also want to create a separate tab for PNC objections, and list every single PNC objection you have ever heard in relation to your product or service. Find a way to organize each objection so you can easily find them – group them by category or separate them with tabs.

Then, list your responses next to each objection – there should be several responses to each objection created with different PNC types in mind. A master list of PNC objections and responses is an invaluable tool for any law firm owner, reception staff or case managers. The more responses you can think of, the better.

Remember, the script binder is never "finished." You will need to make sure that it is updated and added to on a regular basis.

Writing Scripts – Step by Step

Step One: Record What You're Doing Now

If you aren't using scripts – or even if you are – start by recording yourself in action. Use video or audio recording to tape yourself on the phone or in a consultation with a PNC.

Make notes on your body language, word choice, PNC reaction and body language, responses to objections, and closing statements.

You may also wish to ask an associate to make notes on your performance and discuss them with you in a constructive fashion.

Step Two: Evaluate What You're Doing Wrong

Take a look at your notes, and ask yourself the following questions:

- How are you engaging the PNC?
- Are you building common ground and trust?
- Does what you are saying matter to the PNC?
- Is your offer a powerful one?
- What objections are raised?
- How are you dealing with them?
- What objections are you avoiding?
- How natural is your close?
- Are you as effective as you think you can be?

Once you have answered and made notes in response to these questions, make a list of things you need to improve, and how you think you might go about doing so. Do you need to strengthen your closing statements? Do you need to brainstorm more responses to objections? Remember that everyone's script and process can be improved.

Step Three: Decide Who the Script is For

So now that you know the elements of your script you need to work on, you can begin drafting your new script, or revising an old one.

The first part of writing a script – or any piece of marketing material – is having a strong understanding of who you are writing it for. Who is your target audience? Consider demographic characteristics like age, sex, location, income, occupation and marital status. Be as specific as possible. What are their purchase patterns? What motivates them to spend money?

You will want to use words that your target audience will not only understand, but relate to and resonate with. Use sensory language that will trigger emotional and feeling responses – *"I need this"; "This will solve that problem"; " I'll feel better if I have this"*, etc.

Step Four: Decide What You Want to Say

There are typically five sections of every script – and there may be more, depending on the type and purpose of script:

1. Engage

- Get their attention or pique their interest
- Establish common ground
- Build trust, be human
- Thank them for their time

2. Ask + Qualify

- Take control of the conversation by asking questions
- Focus on open-ended questions that cannot be answered with a "yes" or "no"
- Get the PNC talking

- Ask as many questions as you need to get information on the PNC's needs and purchase motivations

3. Get Agreement

- Ask closed-ended questions, if you are sure they will respond with "yes"
- Get them to agree on the benefits of the product or service
- Repeat key points back to the PNC to gain agreement

4. Overcome Objections

- Anticipate objections based on PNC comments, then refute them
- Make informative assumptions about their thought process, identify with their concern, then refute it using your own experiences (tell your story)
- Repeat concerns back to the PNC to let them know you have heard them
- Ask about any remaining objections before you close

5. Close

- Assume that you have overcome all objections, and have the commitment

- Ask the PNC transactional questions, like delivery timing and payment method
- Be as confident and natural as possible

Step Five: Train Your Staff

Once you have written your law firm's scripts, you will need to ensure that your staff understand and are comfortable using them.

Consider having a team meeting, and use role play to review each of the scripts. This will encourage your staff to practice amongst each other, and strengthen their communication skills. Ask them for feedback on the scripts, and make any necessary changes.

You will also need to decide how comfortable you are having your staff personalizing the scripts to suit their own styles. Be clear what elements of the script are "standards" and essential techniques, but also be flexible with your staff.

Step Six: Continually Revise

After you have carefully crafted your script, put it to the test. Practice on your colleagues, friends, and family. Get their feedback, and make changes.

Remember that scripts will need to change and evolve as your law firm changes and evolves, and new products or services are introduced. Keep your script binder on your desk at all times, and continually make changes and improvements to it.

You may also wish to record and evaluate your performance on a regular basis. This is an exercise you could incorporate into regular employee reviews, to use as a constructive tool for staff development.

Script Tips

- Practice anticipating and eliciting real objections – including the ones your PNC doesn't want to raise.

- Make the script yours – it should look, feel, and sound like you naturally do, not like you're reading off the page.

- Spend time with the masters. If there is a person on your reception staff or a case manager you admire in your firm, ask to observe them in action. Take notes on their performance, and the techniques they use for success.

- Don't fear objections. Just spend time identifying as many as possible, then practice overcoming them.

- Never stop thinking of responses to PNC objections. Each objection could potentially have 30 responses, geared toward specific PNC types.

- Anecdotes are persuasive tools – use them in your scripts. People enjoy hearing stories, especially stories that relate to them and their experiences, frustrations, and troubles. Let the story sell your product or service for you.

- Include body language in your scripts – it's just as important as your words. Try mimicking your PNC's posture, arm position, and seating position. This is proven to create ease and build trust.

- If you only have your voice, use it. Pay attention to tone, language choice, speed, and background noise. You only have sound to establish a trusting relationship, so do it carefully.

- Be confident, and focus on a positive stream of self-talk to prepare for the call or consultation. Confidence sells.

- Spend time on your closing scripts, as they are a critical component of your consultation or phone call. This can be a challenging part of the process, so practice, practice, practice.

3

Get Immediate Retainers ("Sales")

If you're a law firm owner, you're also a reception staff or case manager. You've played every role.

You've had to sell the bank to get them to loan you your start-up capital. You've had to sell the best staff and associates on why they should work for your law firm. You've had to convince your law firm partner, spouse, and friends why your law firm idea is a good one.

Now you have to repeatedly sell your product or service to your PNCs.

The ability to convince a PNC to sign with you is a skill that every successful law firm owner has cultivated, and continues to develop. It can be a complicated and time consuming task; one that you will have to continually work on throughout your career in order to be – and stay – successful.

Fortunately, the successful "consultation" is a step-by-step process that can be learned, customized, and continuously improved. There are a wide range of tools available to help and support your efforts.

You don't have to be the most outgoing, enthusiastic person to be successful. You don't even have to be a good speaker. All you need is an understanding of the basic process, and a genuine passion for what you are offering.

"Sales" 101

This is where the law firm process closely aligns with a retail "sales" process. In the next few paragraphs, when I use the word "sales", please assume that I am talking about the PNC consultation that results in getting a retainer fee. As I said before, making sales, or getting a retainer, is a process. There are clear, step-by-step actions that can be taken and result in a PNC becoming a paying PNC.

The process varies according to the type of law firm, type of PNCs and type of product or service that is offered; however, the core steps are the same. Similarly, training varies from individual to individual, but the core skills and abilities remain the same as those used in a retail "sales" process.

Here is a basic seven-step process that you can follow, or fine tune to suit your unique products and services. Remember that each step is important, and builds on the step previous. It is essential to become adept at each step, instead of solely focusing on closing the "sale".

1. Preparation

Make sure you have prepared for your meeting or consultation. You have complete control of this part of the process, so it is important to do everything you can to set the stage for your success.

- Understand your product or service inside and out.
- Prepare all the necessary materials, and organize them neatly.
- Keep your conference room or office tidy and organized.
- Ensure you appear professional and well groomed.
- If possible, do some research on your potential PNC and brainstorm to find common ground.

2. Build a Relationship

The first few minutes you spend with a PNC set the stage for the rest of your interaction. First impressions are everything. Your goal in the second step is to relax the PNC and begin to develop a relationship with them. Establishing a real relationship with your PNC will create trust.

- Make a great first impression: shake hands, make eye contact, and introduce yourself.
- Remain confident and professional, but also personable.
- Mirror their speech and behavior.
- Begin with general questions and small talk.
- Show interest in them.
- Notice and comment on positives.
- Find some common ground on which to relate.

3. Discuss Needs + Wants

Once you have spent a few moments getting to know your PNC, start asking open-ended questions to discover some of their needs and wants. If they have come to you as a "walk in", ask what brought them in to the firm.

- If you are making a holding a consultation or communicating via a phone call, ask for a few moments at the outset to outline the purpose of your visit, as well as how you have structured the communication.
- Listen intently, and repeat back information you are not sure you understand.

- Ask open-ended questions to get them talking. The longer they talk, the more insight they are providing you into their needs and purchase motivations.
- Ask clarifying questions about their responses.

4. Present the Solution

Once you have a solid understanding of what issue the PNC is looking to resolve, you can begin to present the solution: your product or service.

- Explain how your product or service will solve their problem or meet their needs. If several products apply, begin by presenting the mid-level product.
- Illustrate your points with anecdotes about other happy PNCs, or awards the product or service has earned.
- Use hypothetical examples featuring your PNC. Encourage them to picture a scenario after their purchase.
- Begin by describing the benefits of the product, then follow up with features and advantages.
- Watch or listen closely to the PNC's behavior as you speak, and ask further qualifying questions in response to body language and verbal comments.
- Give the PNC an opportunity to ask you questions or provide feedback about each product or service after you have described or explained it.
- Ask closed-ended questions to gain agreement.

5. Overcome Objections

As you present the product or service, take note of potential objections by asking open-ended questions and monitoring body language. Expect that objections will arise and prepare for it. Consider brainstorming a list of all potential objections, and writing down your responses.

- Repeat the objection back to the PNC to ensure you understand them correctly.
- Empathize with what they have said, and then provide a response that overcomes the objection.
- Confirm that the answer you have provided has overcome their objection by repeating yourself.

The Eight Most Common Objections

1. The product or service does not seem valuable to me.
2. There is no reason for me to act know. I will wait.
3. It's safest not to make a decision right away.
4. There is not enough money for the purchase.
5. The competitor or another law firm offers a better product.
6. The relationship with the decision maker is strained.
7. There is an existing contract in place with another law firm.

---

6. Close

This is an important part of the "sales" process that should be handled delicately. Deciding when to close is a judgment call that must be made in the moment during the "sale". Ideally, you have presented a solution to their problem, overcome objections, and have the PNC in a place where they are ready to buy.

Here are some questions to ask before you close am talking about the PNC consultation and getting a retainer fee:

- Does my PNC agree that there is value in my product or service?
- Does my PNC understand the features and benefits of the product or service?
- Are there any remaining objections that must be handled?
- What other factors could influence my PNC's decision to buy?
- Have I minimized the risk involved in the purchase, and provided some level of urgency?

Once you have determined it is time to make the "sale", here are some sample statements you can use to get the process rolling:

- So, should we get started?
- If you just give me your credit card, I can take care of the retainer transaction.
- We can begin immediately if we receive payment by the end of the week.
- Can I email you a draft contract tomorrow?

7. Service + Follow-up

Once you have made the "sale", your work is not over. You want to ensure that that PNC will become a loyal, repeat PNC, and that they will refer their friends to your law firm.

Ask them to be in your PNC database, and keep in touch with regular newsletters. Follow up with a phone call or drop by to ask how they are enjoying the product or service, and if they have any further questions or needs you can assist them with.

This contact opportunity will ensure you are continuing to foster and build a relationship with the PNC- who has now become a paying client.

Up selling

"Up selling" is another term that is firmly entrenched in the retail sales process. However, it can also be applied to your law firm. By simply establishing a relationship with your PNCs to use your law firm for all their legal needs they will choose your firm and spend more money by purchasing additional products or services.

Regardless, "up selling" is an effective way to increase profits and create loyal PNCs – without spending any money to acquire the law new client. These PNCs are already purchasing from you – which means they perceive value in what you have to offer – so take the information you have gained in their previous case process and offer them a little bit more.

You experience up selling on a daily basis. From "do you want fries with that?" to "have you heard about our product protection program?" companies across the globe have tapped into and trained their staff on the value of the up sell.

Up selling is truly rooted in good PNC service. If your PNC purchases a new computer printer, you'll need to make sure they have the cords required to connect it to the computer, regular and photo paper, and color and black and white ink. That is "upselling" and the same principle can be applied to your law firm.

If you don't suggest these items, they may arrive home and realize they do not have all the materials needed to use the product. They may choose to purchase those materials somewhere closer, cheaper, or more helpful.

PNC education is another form of up selling. What if your PNC docsn't realize that you sell a variety of printer paper and stationery in addition to computer hardware like printers? As a law firm, think of this as tax services or criminal law services, family law or juvenile dependency services. Take every opportunity to educate your PNC on the products and services you offer that may be of interest to them.

An effective way of implementing an up sell system into your law firm is simply by creating add-on checklists for the products or services you offer. Each item has a list of related items that your PNC may need. This will encourage your staff to develop the habit of asking for the up sell. This may not always apply to every PNC conversation or consultation, but at least discuss it at a staff meeting so your staff will be aware of it's effectiveness and when to appropriately use it.

Don't forget that another subtle "upsell" strategy is to use your newsletter to educate recipients on the additional products or services that your firm offers.

Team

Employ a strong team of people who will willingly and successfully employ your "sales" strategies.

What Makes a Good Reception person or Case Manager?

There are a lot of people out there looking for receptionist or case manager jobs– but what qualities and skills make a great receptionist or case manager? Remember – when you hire, you're looking for someone with the right "heart". You can always provide training and skills development, but you can't change the "heart". This is something that is learned when a person is 5 or 6 years old, and can't be changed. A good "heart" and the right feeling is going to be so important to a PNC that is in stress because of a legal situation. These "intake" folks have a very critical job – they set the stage for future trust and confidence with your law firm, and ultimately, they begin the process that will hopefully end in the PNC becoming a paying client.   These are additional attributes you will want to find or develop in your team:

- Willingness to continuously learn and improve skills
- Sincerity in relating to PNCs and providing smooth hand offs or solutions to their concerns
- An understanding of the company's big picture
- A communication style that is direct, polite, professional and empathetic
- Honesty and respect for other staff members & associates, PNCs, as well as the competition.
- Ability to manage time
- Enthusiastic
- Inquisitive
- A great listener
- Ability to quickly interpret, analyze, and respond to information during the initial intake process
- Ability to connect and develop relationships of trust with potential PNCs
- Professional appearance

Team Building – Keeping Your Team Together

Effective management of your team is a skill every law firm owner should cultivate. In many law firms, "sales" (aka the intake process) is a department or a whole team of people who work together to generate leads, convert PNCs, and/or smoothly hand off the PNC to a case manager or attorney associate.

Teambuilding, recruitment, and training will be discussed in later sections, but take some time to consider the following aspects of managing a team: (FYI – again, there is a real crossover between the retail "sales" process and your law firm. As a result, wherever you see the word "sales" – think "intake".)

Communication

- Are targets and results regularly reviewed?
- Are opportunities for input regularly provided?
- Do "sales" staff members have a clear understanding of what is expected?
- Do all staff members know daily, weekly, and quarterly targets?

Performance Management

- Are "sales" staff members motivated to reach targets?

1-888-297-1616

- Are "sales" staff recognized and rewarded once those targets are reached?
- Are there opportunities for skills training and development?
- Do staff members have broad and comprehensive product or legal knowledge?
- Is there opportunity for growth within the company?
- Is performance regularly reviewed?

Operations

- Do you have a solid understanding of your "sales" numbers (revenue, profit, margins)?
- Are your "sales" processes regularly reviewed?
- Do you have a variety of "sales" scripts prepared?
- Do you measure conversion rates?
- How are your leads generated?

Intake ("Sales") Tools

Every reception staff or case manager should have an arsenal of tools on hand to assist them in the sales process. These tools can act as aids while a sale is taking place, or help to foster continual learning and development of the reception staff or case manager's skills and approach.

The list below includes some popular sales tools. Add to this list with other resources that are specific to your law firm or industry.

Tool	Description + Benefit
Scripts	Create several different scripts throughout your law firm Maintains consistency in your sales approach Revise and renew your scripts regularly
Presentation Materials or "leave behinds"	High-quality information about your product or service Forms: PowerPoint presentation, brochure, product sheets, books, etc. Serves as an outline of your sales presentation, and keeps you on task
Colleagues	A source of help and advice, especially when you are on the same team Also a source of support
PNC Databases	An accurate, up-to-date database of PNC contact information and contact history Used to stay in touch with PNCs Can also be used for direct mail and follow-up telemarketing, or as a contact "list" for e-mail marketing – aka newsletters.
The Internet	A powerful resource for sales help and advice – for example, your law firm website is a good source of helpful information Source for product knowledge – again your law firm website(s)
Ongoing Training	Constant improvement of your sales skills Constant increase in product knowledge Investment in yourself and your company

8 Tips for Better "Sales"

- **Dress for the sale.** Dress professionally, appear well put together and maintain good hygiene. Ensure you are not only dressed professionally, but *appropriately*. Would your PNC feel more comfortable if you wore a suit, or jeans and blazer?

- **Speak their language.** Show you understand their needs or culture, and use phrases your PNC understands. This may require researching industry jargon or common phrases. Remember to avoid using words and phrases that are used in the legal process. Doing so will help "level the playing field between the PNC and the experts" in your law firm.

- **Ooze positivity**. Show up or answer the phone with a smile, and leave your personal issues behind. Be enthusiastic about what you have to offer, and how that offering will benefit your PNC. Reflect this not only in your voice, but also in your body language.

- **Deliver a strong pitch or presentation**. Be confident and convincing. Leave self-doubt at the door, and walk in assuming the sale. Take time to explain complex concepts, and always connect what you're saying to your PNC in a specific way.

- **Be a poster-child for good manners**. Accept any amenity you're offered, listen intently, don't interrupt, don't show up late, have a strong handshake, and give everyone you are speaking to equal attention.

- **Avoid sensitive subjects**. Politics, religion, swearing, sexual innuendos and racial comments are absolutely off-limits. So are negative comments about other PNCs or the competition.

- **Create a real relationship.** Icebreakers and small talk are not just to pass the time before the business part of your communication. They are how relationships get established. Show genuine interest in everything your PNC has to say. Ask questions about topics you know they are passionate. Speak person to person, not reception staff or case managers to PNC. Remember everything. Make notes that will help facilitate a smooth handoff to the next person in the process that speaks to the PNC. This is known as the "heart/head" model. You begin the conversation with the heart, and then move to the business, then move back to the heart, back to business, and so on.

- **Know more than you need to.** Impress PNCs with comprehensive knowledge – not only of your product or service – but also of the people who use that product or service, and competition trends. Be seen as an expert in order to build trust and respect.

4

Double your Referrals

What if I told you that you could put an inexpensive system in place that would effectively allow your law firm to grow itself?

For most law firm owners, a large part of their PNC base is comprised of referral PNCs. These people found out about the law firms products or services from the recommendation of a friend or colleague who had a positive experience working with your law firm.

If your law firm benefits from referral PNCs, you will find that these PNCs arrive ready to buy from you, and tend to buy more often. They also tend to be highly loyal to your product or service.

Seems like great PNCs to have, right?

Referral PNCs cost less to acquire. Compared to the leads you generate from advertising, direct mail campaigns, and other marketing initiatives, referral PNCs come to you already qualified and already trusting in the quality of your offering and the respectability of your staff.

With a little effort, and the creation of a formalized system – or strategy – you can not only continue to benefit from referrals to your law firm, but easily double the number of referral PNCs that walk through your door. All of this is possible for a minimal investment of time and resources.

Is Your Law firm a Referral Law firm?

Referral based law firms benefit from a stream of qualified PNCs who arrive at their doorstep ready to sign a contract and submit a retainer fee. These law firms put less focus on advertising to generate new leads, and more focus on serving and communicating with their existing PNCs.

Generally speaking, a referral program can generate outstanding results for nearly any law firm. Since most referrals do not require any effort, the addition of a strategy and a program will often double or triple the number of qualified referrals that come through a law firm door.

A referral program can:

- **Save you time**. Referral strategies – once established – don't require much management or time investment.

- **Deliver more qualified PNCs**. Your PNC arrives with an assumption of trust, and willing to purchase.
- **Improve your reputation.** Your PNC's networks likely overlap, and create potential for a single PNC to be referred by two people. This encourages the perception that your law firm is "the place to go."
- **Speed the sales process.** You will have existing common ground and a reputation with the referred PNC.

- **Increase your profit.** You will spend less time and money generating leads, and more time serving PNCs who have their wallets open.

The Cost of Your PNCs

As we discussed in the "Repeat Law firm" section, you don't "get" PNCs, you *buy* them. The money you spend on advertising, direct mail, and other promotions ideally results in potential PNCs walking through your doors.

For example, if you placed an ad for $200, and 20 people make a purchase in response to that ad, you would have paid $10 for each PNC.

Referral PNCs cost you next to nothing. Your existing PNC does the work of selling your law firm to their friend or associate, and you benefit from the sale. Aside from the cost of any referral incentives, there is no cost involved at all.

Referral PNCs cost less and require less time investment than any other PNC. That means you can spend that time making them a loyal PNC, or a devoted fan.

Groom Your PNCs

Referral strategies can allow you to groom your PNC base. As we have previously discussed, 80% of your revenue comes from 20% of your PNCs – these are your ideal PNCs.

These are also the people you have established as your target market, and are the people you cater your marketing and advertising efforts toward.

You also have a group of PNCs who make up 80% of your headaches. These are the people who complain the most and spend the least.

Use your referral strategy to get more of your *ideal* PNCs. Spend more time servicing your ideal client – do everything you can to make them happy – and less time on your headache clients.

Then, focus your referral efforts on your ideal PNCs. Ask

them to refer other PNC's to you, and reward them for doing so. Try to avoid referrals from your headache PNCs – chances are you'll just get another headache.

Referral Sources

Take some time to brainstorm all the people who could potentially refer to you. Think beyond your law firm, to your extracurricular activities and personal life. There are endless sources of people who are ready and willing to send potential PNCs your way.

Here are some ideas to get you started:

Past Relationships

No, not romantic relationships. I'm talking about anyone you have previously had a relationship with, but for one reason or another have fallen out of touch. This includes former colleagues, associates, PNCs and friends.

Including them in your referral strategy can be as simple as reaching out through the phone or email, and updating them on your latest law firm initiative or career move. Gently ask at the end of the correspondence to refer anyone who may need your product or service. They will appreciate that you have attempted to re-establish the relationship. Another way to do this is to ask a person (relationship) if they would be willing to be on your e-mail list. Then, no matter how long it's been since you've had face-to-face communication, you're always staying "top of mind" and "in touch" with your past relationships via your newsletters and/or direct mail marketing pieces.

Suppliers and Vendors

Your suppliers and vendors can be a great source for referrals, because they presumably deal daily with law firms that are complementary to your own. The opportunities to connect two of their contacts in a mutually beneficial relationship are endless. .

Clients

Your current and/or previous clients are an obvious source of referrals, because they are the people who are dealing with you directly on a regular basis.

Your clients also have a high level of product knowledge when it comes to your law firm, and are in a great position to really sell the strength of your company. Remember from the Testimonials section - the words of your clients are at least 10 times more powerful than any clever headline or marketing piece you could create.

Employees and Associates

Give your employees and associates a reason to have their friends and families investigate your law firm with a simple incentive program. These people have the most product knowledge, and are in the best position to sell you to a PNC.

This is also a way to tap into an endless network of people. Who do your employees and associates know? Who do their friends and friends of friends know? A referral chain that connects to your employees can be a highly powerful one.

Competitors

This doesn't seem so obvious, but it can work. Your direct competitors are clearly not the ideal source for referrals. However, indirect competitors can refer their PNCs or potential PNCs to you if they cannot meet those PNCs' needs themselves.

For example, if you sell high end lighting fixtures, the low-budget lighting store down the street may be able to refer PNCs to you, and vice versa. You may wish to offer a finder's fee or incentive to establish this arrangement.

Your Network

Don't be shy about asking your friends and family members – even your competition - for referrals. To apply this concept to the legal industry, you know as well as anyone, that not all law firms are experts in every facet of the law. The law firm down the street may be an expert in handling family law cases, but they don't have experts – like you – in juvenile dependency. So, it makes sense to develop a "referral" relationship with this particular competitor. You could even provide your friends and family – or your competition - with an incentive – a gift, a meal, or a portion of the sale.

Associations + Special Interest Groups

This is another place you likely have a network of people who have limited knowledge about what you do or what your law firm does. The advantage here is that you have a group of people with similar beliefs and values in the same room. Use it!

The Media

Unless a member of the media is a regular client of yours, and thus presents a conflict of interest, the opportunity here is to establish a relationship with an editor or journalist, and position yourself as an expert in your area or legal expertise. Then, next time they are writing a related story, they can ask to quote you and your opinion. When their audience reads the story, they will perceive your law firm as the industry leader.

Referral Strategies

A referral strategy is any system you can put in place to generate new leads through existing clients. The ideal way to do this is to create a system that runs itself! Here are some ideas for simple strategies you can begin to implement into your law firm immediately.

Just Ask

This may seem simple and obvious, but it's true. Be open with your PNCs and associates, and simply ask them if they can refer any of their friends or associates to you. Make it part of doing law firm with you, and your PNCs will grow to expect the question. Or, let them know in advance that you'll be asking at a later date.

Remember that this can include potential PNCs – even if they don't buy from you. The reason they chose not to purchase may have nothing to do with your law firm; any person who has begun to or actually done law firm with you can refer to you another person.

Offer Incentives

When you speak to your PNCs, when you ask them for something, you typically try to answer the question "what's in it for me?" before they ask it.

The same is true when you ask your PNCs for a referral. Incentive-based referral strategies work wonders, and can easily be implemented as part of a PNC loyalty program, or as part of your existing PNC relations systems.

Consider offering PNCs who successfully refer PNCs to you discounts on products, free products or services, or gifts. Offer incentives relative to the number of referrals, or the success rate of each referral.

This can have a spin off effect, as your referral PNCs may become motivated to continue the referral chain. They too will be interested in the incentives you have provided, and tell their friends about your law firm.

Be Proactive

The only way your referral program will work is if you put some effort into it, and maintain some level of ongoing effort.
Here are some ideas:

- Put a referral card or coupon in every shopping bag that leaves your store
- Promote gift certificates during peak seasons
- Offer free information seminars to existing PNCs, and ask them to bring a friend
- Host a closed-door sale for your top 20 PNCs and their friends

Provide Great PNC Service

An easy way to encourage referral law firm is to treat every potential PNC with exemplary PNC service. Since the art of PNC service is lost is many communities, people are often impressed by simple added touches and conveniences. That alone will encourage them to refer your law firm to their network.

Stay in Touch

Make sure you are staying in touch with all of your potential and converted PNCs. Through newsletters, direct mail, or the Internet, keep your law firm name at the top of the minds, ahead of the competition.

Even if they have already purchased from you, and may not need to purchase for some time, a newsletter or email can be a simple reminder that your law firm is out there. If someone in their network is looking for the product or service, it will be more likely that your PNC will refer your law firm over the competition.

5

Profit Over the Phone

For some, the word 'telemarketing' brings up images of rows of people with headsets, all working from a head office in a country far, far away.

Others think of the people who always seem to call the minute they take their first bite of dinner. Some just think it's an old fashioned marketing strategy. While in some cases this may be true, telemarketing is still an important tool for every law firm – of every size.

What if I were to tell you that you were *already* using telemarketing as a regular part of your law firm? In my opinion, telemarketing is re-emerging as a powerful way to generate leads and close sales. Done well, it's also efficient and cost-effective.

Every time the people who work your front end pick up the

phone, they're engaging in a telemarketing process. Every time one of your attorneys returns a phone call to a client, they too are engaging in a telemarketing process.

Telemarketing is not just a system for cold calls. It's any type of formal communication between your company and its PNCs or clients over the phone.

So, now you know that you're already doing it, let's talk about how to turn telemarketing into a profitable marketing strategy for your law firm.

Telemarketing for Your Law firm

A common misconception is that telemarketing needs to happen on a broad scale in order to be effective. Pages and pages of potential PNCs must be cold called on a daily basis. Law firms must hire dozens of staff members to conduct and manage the efforts.

Like I mentioned above, telemarketing is any kind of formal communication that happens between a company and a potential new client (PNC)l or existing client over the phone. Regardless of the size of your law firm, you can train your existing staff members to effectively use the telephone to generate more leads and convert more sales.

The benefits of establishing an organized telemarketing system are:

- Instant access. Reach key decision-makers immediately.
- One-on-one interaction. Develop real relationships with empathy and trust.
- Minimal cost. Spend less on sales outreach and research.

Who are the Best Telemarketers?

Success in telemarketing has a lot to do with the personality of your company's representative. Generally, good telemarketers have the following qualities and abilities:

- Energy and enthusiasm
- Positive attitude
- Good phone manner
- Empathy
- Belief in your company and its products
- Strong listening skills
- Ability to think on-the-spot
- Ability to handle objection and rejection
- Good organizational skills

The Telemarketing Process

There are two types of telemarketing: outgoing and incoming. You should have a proactive strategy in place to handle both types.

Remember that your approach to telemarketing must have a clear objective; a clear purpose. What is the purpose of the call (outgoing and incoming)? Is it to inform? Set up an appointment? Establish a need or desire? Give out information? Provide an update? This will help guide how you handle each type.

Incoming Calls

When a PNC calls your law firm for the first time, you should have a system in place to make a great, PNC service-oriented impression. Many of these PNCs will have seen one of your advertisements, received a direct mail piece, visited a website, or be responding to any other element of your marketing campaign.

Your telemarketing strategy for incoming phone calls can take the form of:

- An answering service
- Voice mail
- A messaging service
- A quick, case assessment and warm handoff
- An information provision system

The person – or people – who answer incoming calls should be well trained for the role and clearly understand the expectations for handling them. Your receptionist should be trained thoroughly in the types of cases and caller needs so he/she can answer basic PNC questions intelligently. Your team should know how to answer the phone according to your company policy, and have excellent phone manners.

Consider including the following instructions into your incoming telemarketing system or process:

- Answer the phone after two and before four rings
- Have a standard company greeting. Include your company name, **as well as the name of the person answering the phone.**
- Ensure sufficient PNC information is recorded. Determine what information is important to gain from each caller – develop a simple Excel spreadsheet to collect name, phone number, reason for call, action required, who is responsible for following up
- Do not place anyone on hold for longer than 20 seconds. Instead, take their name and number and have their call returned promptly.
- Establish a short description of your company's process or point of difference at some point during the phone call.
- Always repeat back any information or agreement exchanged.
- Be the last one to hang up.

Outgoing Calls

Outgoing calls are the more challenging aspect of your telemarketing strategy. In this case you are proactively asking your PNC/client for something, as opposed to responding once they've already been convinced to act.

You can use an outgoing telemarketing strategy to:

- Set appointments
- Update databases
- Follow up on direct mail and other campaigns
- Conduct surveys

Your outgoing phone call needs to engage the person on the other end, and begin to build a relationship based solely on verbal communication (i.e., without the assistance of non-verbal cues and behaviors). Depending on the type of call, you will be seeking to:

- Attract their attention
- Spark their interest, needs, or desires
- Motivate them to act
- Seek agreement

It is essential to the success of your outgoing telemarketing efforts that you create a script for each type of outgoing call your company makes. This will keep you – and your staff – focused on the purpose of the call and give you tools and prompts to keep you on track. We will review scripts for telemarketing later in this chapter.

Here are some simple steps for making your outgoing telemarketing efforts a success:

Know who you are calling

Do your research. Know exactly who it is you need to contact. Is it a PNC or existing client? Once you know who you are targeting, you can do some research prior to your phone call, and ensure you call at a time that is convenient. You will want to know a bit about their interests or existing case as well as their role within the family structure. If you have served another client with the same type of case, let them know.

When you have them on the phone, confirm that the basic information you have is correct (name, title, etc.). Make sure you speak with the person who is designated as the "spokesperson" for the case or the decision-maker.

Be prepared; stay organized

Have all the materials you may need in front of you, and clear your desk of any distractions. Have a notepad handy, and record key elements of the conversation for action or later discussion. Also, keep a record of all the calls you make, and the results of each call. This will prevent you from making duplicate calls, which do not reflect well on your organization, as well as track left messages and the most productive times of the day for outgoing phone calls.

Know why you are calling

Like I mentioned above, your phone calls should be purpose-focused. Are you calling to set up a meeting? Introduce yourself and develop an initial strategy? Request that they make payment on an outstanding invoice? Get them to sign a critical document? Keep this clear in your mind and stick to it.?

Use strong phone skills

You can create a great first impression on the phone when you cultivate great phone communication skills. Pay attention to the tone of your voice, whether or not you are smiling, the pacing of your sentences (slower is better), and general phone manners. Ensure you clearly identify who you are and what law firm you work for every time you speak to someone new.

Telemarketing Scripts

Scripts are essential to successful telemarketing. You and your employees will benefit having a "plan of action" for every type of phone call that your company makes. This will also ensure that each staff member has a consistent approach, which is part of your branding.

We discussed the importance of scripts and writing scripts earlier in the program, but I encourage you to review the section before you craft your telemarketing scripts.

Here is a list of components you will need to include in your scripts:

Greeting: Opening the Conversation

Your incoming calls should be handled with a consistent, friendly greeting that informs the PNC of what law firm (or department) they've reached and who they're talking to.

Outgoing calls need to engage the PNC/client within the first few moments, just as a headline needs to catch the reader's instant attention. Say just enough to pique their interest and keep them listening, then begin to explain why you are calling.

The opening conversation should be simple and focused on developing a relationship. Ask casual questions and use small talk to put the caller at ease, but don't go on too long. You don't want to appear to be wasting their time.

Reason for your Call

If someone asks why you are calling, tell them. Be up front about why you are calling; clearly state your objectives, then back them up with an explanation that includes benefits to the PNC (or positive outcomes for their case) or to the existing client.

You may wish to ask permission before you get into an explanation. Asking, "do you mind if I tell you exactly why I called today?" shows respect for the PNC's/client's time, and gives them an opportunity to agree to listen.

You may also wish to outline exactly what you're going to cover during the call. Again, ask them if you can go over this information with them. This will show that you have given the phone call substantial thought, organized your information, and respect their time.

Asking Questions

Information gathering is an essential component of both incoming and outgoing telemarketing. (This section is most relevant to your intake personnel and/or case managers, and, most likely will occur with a potential new client.) Ask as many questions as possible, and encourage your PNC to start talking. This will keep you in control of the conversation. Even if the questions don't relate specifically to the matter at hand, your PNC's response may provide information that will add to your case manager's ability to convert a PNCs general interest in your firm to becoming an actual, paying client.

For incoming calls, listen to the PNC's question, then ask if you can take a moment to ask them some questions before you answer theirs. This will allow you to explain your company's process, ask the PNC some qualifying questions, and gain control of the conversation.

You will want to also consider asking questions related to the following topics:

- **Responsibility** – Who is in charge of making the decision? Is it the same person who will be financially responsible?
- **Budget** – How much financial resource is available for your service? What is the budget? (Is their some component of the case your firm can manage that will better meet their budget)? Is this the time to set up a meeting for a free consultation?
- **Timeframe** – When does the PNC need the service? What is the reason for these deadlines? (I'm assuming that the need here is always "immediate".)
- **Competition** – Who else is the PNC talking to? What will impact their decision? What aspects are they comparing?

Closed-ended questions

Closed-ended questions are not the best way to get your PNC talking, but they do provide information quickly and succinctly. Closed-ended questions are questions that can be answered with one word – usually "yes" or "no".

Open-ended questions

Open-ended questions are just that: they cannot be answered in one word. These are great questions to use for the majority of your telemarketing because they encourage the PNC to provide explanations, giving the case manager insight into their needs and opinions.

Obtaining Agreement

At key points throughout the conversation, you will need to ensure you are on the same page as your PNC. You will need to find a way to get feedback from your caller on what you have been saying.

An easy way to do this is to ask them a question you are sure they'll say yes to. Something like, "so what I'm hearing, is that you feel you've ben wronged, and you need a remedy as soon as possible." or "I'm sure you would agree that you need the best and would benefit from retaining our firm."

Encouraging them to agree with you strengthens your argument, and leads directly to the sale. It's a powerful method of persuasion.

Overcoming Objections

This will be the most challenging component of your script – largely because you do not know for sure what your PNC's objections are going to be. You will have to think in the moment, and attempt to overcome each objection in a calm, professional way.

Before you pick up the phone, you may wish to brainstorm all potential objections, and think of your ideal response. A simple chart that looks like this will be a helpful tool to refer to during your call:

Potential Objection	Response

Remember to respect the objections as they are raised, and treat each point your PNC makes as a legitimate one. Show empathy and relate to what they have to say. Phrases like "I can see how that would be a concern for you..." "I used to think the same thing..." and "Sure, that's completely understandable..." allow you to relate to them, establish common ground, and then share how you overcame your own objections.

Closing with Commitment

Once you have opened the conversation, developed a relationship, asked questions, secured agreement, and overcome objections, all you have to do is close the conversation with a commitment.

The commitment should be your objective for calling, or a step toward that objective. For example, if the purpose of your call was to set up a meeting, ensure that you commit to a time and place before you end the conversation.

Assume that if you have gotten this far, you have the sale. Be confident, and use phrases like, "How about we meet on this day at this time…"

You will want to confirm whatever you have committed to in writing with your PNC. If you have set an appointment, send them a quick note to thank them for the phone call, and put the meeting in writing. Remember to be as polite and succinct as possible. Avoid lengthy emails and letters.

Tips for Effective Telemarketing

Communicating with your existing clients and PNCs over the phone requires a different set of skills than in-person communication. Make sure you choose the best people for this job – when you only have your voice to communicate, you must be extra aware of the impression you give the person on the other line.

Smile

This may seem like a silly point to put at the top of this list, but it is important. Your caller will be able to hear if you are smiling, and interpret your smile as your enthusiasm or interest in speaking with them. You will sound more positive, friendly, and open to dialogue. Remember, the person on the other line can hear *everything*, so avoid multi-tasking (drinking, eating, unnecessary typing) when you're on the phone.

Be a good listener

Once you get your PNC talking – listen. They will be giving you important insight into their financial concerns, and their potential objections. Take notes as you listen, and never assume you know what they are going to say. After long periods of speech, check in and repeat back what you have heard to confirm you have heard it properly. Make sure to leave a pause between what they have just said, and what you are about to say. This shows that you have been listening and are not jumping in at your first opportunity.

Call at an optimal time

Knowing who you are calling will ensure that you contact them at the most appropriate time – the time they are most likely to answer your phone call. For example, law firm owners will need to be reached during law firm hours. Try to reach them during quiet times – usually first thing in the morning, or right before close. If you are calling PNCs or existing clients, then make your calls in the evening when they are most likely to be home, or as specified in their contact information.

Use a familiar tone

You only have your voice to establish a new relationship with a potential PNC. The tone you choose is just as important – and has just as much impact – as the words you choose. Use a tone that is friendly and confident, and resembles the way you would speak to your friends.

A Profit Manual for Attorneys

Be prepared to handle rejection

No matter how targeted your contact list, how amazing your script, how great your approach, rejection is an inevitable part of outgoing telemarketing. Your telemarketers are going to have to become very skilled at handling rejection. In fact, some people will not only reject what you have to say, they'll be rude in doing so. Remember not to take this personally – they could be having a bad day, or just not have enough time to listen to what you have to say. Consider asking to call back at a better time – or just shrug it off.

Be prepared to handle difficult PNCs

Difficult PNCs and existing clients will appear on the other end of the phone line – for both incoming and outgoing calls. This is another inevitability of telemarketing, and for law firms, in general. Again, remember not to take what they have to say personally – they just want to air their frustrations and be heard. Listen intently, stay calm, and try to empathize with what they have to say. Never interrupt, use calming language, and record as much as possible about what they are saying. Then, either promise to follow up – allowing yourself to take time to consider how you would like to handle the problem – to try to resolve their issue immediately. A trick I've learned over the years, is that in order to "de-escalate" and angry or frustrated caller is to tell them that "I'm taking notes", and I will periodically stop them and repeat back to them what they are saying, because I want to correctly capture their concerns.

Make the call standing up

When you are standing, you will sound my confident, authoritative, and decisive. Your diaphragm is expanded when you are standing, which will increase the confidence in your voice. Do this for the critical cases and important phone calls.

Have strong phone manners

Here are some tips for ensuring you have a strong, professional phone presence:

- Introduce yourself with your full name
- State your law firm's name
- Then, ask for the contact by name
- Tell them why you are calling
- If you do not reach your PNC/client, ask for a more convenient time
- Do not hold, call back instead (your time is valuable, too!)

6

Generate Unlimited Leads for Your Law Firm

Where do your PNCs come from?

Most people would probably choose advertising as an answer. Or referrals. Or direct mail campaigns. This may seem true, but it's not really accurate.

Your PNCs come from leads that have been turned into sales. Each PNC goes through a two-step process before they arrive with their wallets open. They have been converted from a member of a target market, to a lead, then to a client.

So, would it not stand to reason then, that when you advertise or send any marketing material out to your target market, that you're not really trying to generate clients? That instead, you're trying to generate leads.

When you look at your marketing campaign from this perspective, the idea of generating leads as compared to clients seems a lot less daunting. The pressure of closing sales is no longer placed on advertisements or brochures.

From this perspective, the **general purpose of your advertising and marketing efforts is then to generate leads from qualified PNCs.** Seems easy enough, doesn't it?

Where Are Your Leads Coming From?

If I asked you to tell me the top three ways you generate new sales leads, what would you say?

- Advertising?
- Word of mouth?
- Networking?
- ...don't know?

The first step toward increasing your leads is in understanding how many leads you currently get on a regular basis, as well as where they come from. Otherwise, how will you know when you're getting more phone calls or walk-in PNCs?

If you don't know where your leads come from, start *today*. Start asking every PNC that comes through your door, "how did you hear about us?" or "what brought you in today?" Ask every PNC that calls where they found your telephone number, or email address. Then, *record the information for at least an entire week.*

When you're finished, take a look at your spreadsheet and write your top three lead generators here:

1. _____

2. _____

3. _____

After being in business for a short time, I decided to grow my law firm. Using the above method, I found that my best "leads" came from my existing clients. I was very successful in growing my law firm. Now that I'm writing this book, and recalling how successful this tracking method was, I realize that I need to get back to this process.

From Lead to PNC: Conversion Rates

Leads mean nothing to your law firm unless you convert them into paying clients. You could get hundreds of leads from a single advertisement, but unless those leads result in a retainer, it's been a largely unsuccessful (and costly) campaign.

The ratio of leads (potential PNCs) to transactions (actual clients) is called your conversion rate. Simply divide the number of PNCs who actually paid a retainer by the number of PNCs who inquired about your service, and multiply by 100.

 # transactions (actual paying clients) / # leads (PNCs) x 100 = % conversion rate

If, in a given week, I have 879 PNCs come into my office, and 143 of them become paying clients, the formula would look like this:

[143 (paying clients) / 879 (PNCs)] x 100 = 16.25% conversion rate

What's Your Conversion Rate?

Based on the formula above, you can see that the higher your conversion rate, the more profitable the law firm.

Your next step is to determine you own current conversion rate. Add up the number of leads you sourced in the last section, and divide that number into the total transactions that took place in the same week.

Write your conversion rate here:

_____.

Quality (or Qualified) Leads

Based on our review of conversion rates, we can see that the number of leads you generate means nothing unless those leads are being converted into paying clients.

So what affects your ability (and the ability of your team) to turn leads into clients? Do you need to improve your scripts? Your product or service? Find a more competitive edge in the marketplace?

Maybe. But the first step toward increasing conversion rates is to evaluate the leads you are currently generating, and make sure those leads are the right ones.

What are Quality Leads?

Potential PNCs are potential PNCs, right? Anyone who walks into your store or picks up the phone to call your law firm could be convinced to hire you, right? Not necessarily, but this is a common assumption most law firm owners make.

Quality leads are the people who are the most likely to hire you. They are the qualified buyers who comprise your target market. Let's use an example from a "retail" industry: For example, anyone might walk in off the street to browse a furniture store – regardless of whether or not they are in the market for a new couch or bed frame.

This lead is solely interested in browsing, and is not likely to be converted to a purchaser.

A quality lead would be someone looking for a new kitchen table, and who specifically drove to that same furniture because a friend had raved about the service they received that month. **These are the kinds of leads you need to focus on generating.**

How Do You Get Quality Leads?

- **Know your target market**. Get a handle on who your PNCs are – the people who are most likely to buy your product or service. Know their age, sex, income, and purchase motivations. From that information you can determine how best to reach your specific audience.

- **Focus on the 80/20 rule**. A common statistic in law firms is that 80% of your revenue comes from 20% of your PNCs. These are your star PNCs, or your ideal PNCs. These are the PNCs you should focus your efforts on recruiting. This is the easiest way to grow your law firm and your income.

- **Get specific.** Focus not only on who you want to attract, but how you're going to attract them. If you're trying to generate leads from a specific market segment, craft a unique offer to get their attention.

- **Be proactive**. Once you've generated a slew of leads, make sure you have the resources to follow up on them. Be diligent and aggressive, and follow up in a timely manner. You've done to work to get them, now reel them in.

Get More Leads from Your Existing Strategies

Increasing your lead generation doesn't necessarily mean diving in and implementing an expensive array of new marketing strategies. Marketing and any type of outreach for the purpose of lead generation can be inexpensive, and bring a high return on investment.

You are likely already implementing many of these strategies. With a little tweaking or refinement, you can easily double your leads, and ensure they are more qualified.

Here are some popular ways to generate quality leads:

Direct Mail to Your Ideal PNCs

Direct mail is one of the fastest and most effective ways to generate leads that will build your law firm. It's a simple strategy – in fact, you're probably already reaching out to your target market through direct mail letters with enticing offers.

The secret to doubling your results is to craft your direct mail campaigns specifically for a highly targeted audience of your *ideal* PNCs.

Your ideal PNCs are the people who will be most likely to hire you. They are the PNCs who will hire you over and over again, and refer your law firm to their friends. They are the group of 20% of your PNCs who make up 80% of your revenue.

Identify your ideal PNCs

Who are your ideal PNCs? What is their age, sex, income, location and purchase motivation? Where do they live? How do they spend their money? Be as specific as possible.

Once you have identified who your ideal PNCs are, you can begin to determine how you can go about reaching them. Will you mail to households or apartment buildings? Families or retirees? Direct mail lists are available for purchase from a wide range of companies, and can be segregated into a variety of demographic and sociographic categories.

Craft a special offer

Create an offer that's too good to refuse – not for your entire target market, but for your ideal PNC. How can you cater to their unique needs and wants? What will be irresistible for them?

Let's use that same "retail" experience: For example, if you operate a furniture store, your target market is a broad range of people. However, if you are targeting young families, your offer will be much different than one you may craft for empty-nesters.

Court them for your law firm

Don't stop at a single mail-out. Sometimes people will throw your letter away two or three times before they are motivated to act. Treat your direct mail campaign like a courtship, and understand that it will happen over time.

First send a letter introducing yourself, and your irresistible offer. Then follow up on a monthly basis with additional letters, newsletters, offers, or flyers. Repetition and reinforcement of your presence is how your PNC will go from saying, "who is this law firm" to "I use this law firm."

Advertise for lead generation

Statistics show that nearly 50% of all purchase decisions are motivated by advertising. It can also be a relatively cost effective way of generating leads.

We've already discussed the importance of ensuring your advertisements are purpose-focused. The general purpose of most advertisements is to increase sales – which starts with leads. However ads that are created solely for lead generation – that is, to get the PNCs to pick up the phone or walk in the office – are a category of their own.

Lead generation ads are simply designed to create a sense of curiosity or mystery. Often, they feature an almost unbelievable offer. Their purpose is not to convince the PNC to hire you, but to contact the law firm for more information.

As always, when you are targeting your ideal audience, you'll need to ensure that your ads are placed prominently in publications that your audience reads. This doesn't mean you have to fork over the cash for expensive display ads. Inexpensive advertising in e-mail newsletters, and classifieds, are very effective for lead generation.

Tips for lead generation advertising:

Leverage low-cost advertising

Place ads in the yellow pages, classifieds section, e-mail newsletters, and online. If your target audience is technology savvy, consider new forms of advertising like Facebook and Google Adwords.

For example, I have an advertisement in the yellow pages. I know this is an old-fashioned, low tech means of marketing. However, I just recently got a testimonial from a client who said he initially "found" me by opening the phone book and calling the firm that had the biggest and most pleasing advertisement. I've had this advertisement in the yellow pages for years, but the revenue generated from this one paying client paid for the yellow pages ad many times over.

Spark curiosity

Don't give them all the information they need to make a decision. Ask them to contact you for the full story, or the complete details of the seemingly outrageous offer.

Grab them with a killer headline

Like all advertising, a compelling headline is essential. Focus on the greatest benefits to the PNC, or feature an unbelievable offer. For example, I have an e-mail marketing system, and the person who manages these e-mails tells me that she spends more time figuring out the "headline" for the e-mail marketing campaign than she does actually developing the content of the e-mail.

Referrals and host beneficiary relationships

A referral system is one of the most profitable systems you can create in your law firm. The beauty is once it's set up, it often runs itself.

PNCs that come to you through referrals are often your "ideal PNCs." They are already trusting and willing to buy. This is one of the most cost-effective methods of generating new law firm, and is often the most profitable. These referral PNCs will buy more, faster, and refer further law firm to your company. As I said earlier in this chapter, I found that this is so true. My best referrals always come from my existing clients

Referrals naturally happen without much effort for reputable law firms, but with a proactive referral strategy you'll certainly double or triple your referrals. Sometimes, you just need to ask!

Here are some easy strategies you can begin to implement today:

Referral incentives

Give your clients a reason to refer their friends and/or acquaintances to you. Reward them with discounts, gifts, or free service in exchange for a successful referral.

Referral program

Offer new PNCs a free product or service to get them in the door. Then, at the end of the transaction – after they hire you - , give them three more 'coupons' for the same free product or service that they can give to their friends. Do the same with their friends. This ongoing program will bring you more clients than you can imagine.

Host-beneficiary relationships

Forge alliances with non-competitive companies who target your ideal PNCs. Create cross-promotion and cross-referral direct mail campaigns that benefit both your law firm and the business "down the street".

Lead Management Systems

Once your lead generation strategies are in place, you'll also need a system to manage incoming inquiries. You'll need to ensure you receive enough information from each lead to follow up on it at a later date. You'll also need to create a system to organize that information, and track the lead as it is converted into a sale.

Gathering Information from Your Leads

Here is a list of information you should gather from your leads. This list can be customized to the needs of your law firm, and the type of information you can realistically ask for from your potential PNCs.

- Company Name
- Name of Contact
- Alternate Contact Person
- Mailing Address
- Phone Number
- Fax Number
- Cell Phone
- Email Address

- Website Address
- Product of Interest
- Mailing Address
- Phone Number
- Fax Number
- Cell Phone
- Other Competitors Engaged

Lead List Management Methods:

Once you have gathered information from your lead, you'll need a system to organize their information and keep a detailed contact history.

The simplest way to do this is with a database program, but you can also use a variety of hard copy methods.

Electronic Database Programs

- High level of organization available
- Unlimited space for notes and record-keeping
- Data-entry required
- Examples include: MS Outlook, MS Excel, Maximizer
- Customer Relationship Management Software

Index Cards

- Variety of sizes: 3x5, 4x6 or 5x8
- Basic contact information on one side
- Notes on the other side
- Easy to organize and sort

Rolodex System

- Maintain more contacts than index card system
- Easily organized and compact

- Basic contact information on one side
- Notes on the other side
- Can keep phone conversation and purchase details

Notebook

- Best if leads are managed by a single person
- Lots of room for notes
- Inexpensive
- Difficult to re-organize
- Best for smaller lists

Law firm Card Organizer

- Best for small lists – under 100
- Limited space for notes
- No data entry required
- Rolodex-style, or clear binder pages

7

Get Leads from Host-Beneficiary Relationships

Did you know that a law firm or retail business just down the street from yours may be able to help double your profits this year? Or does this sound a little too far-fetched?

Maybe. If you operate a retail store that sells tires, and the business down the road is a hair salon, you may have a hard time making this happen. However, loose partnerships between complementary, non-competing law firms can be a financial goldmine when implemented strategically. And your partner may be just steps away!

Formally called Host Beneficiary Relationships, these partnerships help small and medium-sized law firms tap into very specific target markets and close sales under existing relationships of trust.

HB Relationships allow one law firm (the 'host') to add value to their product or service, and the other (the 'beneficiary') to benefit from the impact of a referral. The beauty of this arrangement is that the roles can then be swapped; the 'host' becomes the 'beneficiary' and vice versa.

Like any marketing strategy, HB Relationships don't work for every law firm all the time. However, they are a great tool to keep in your marketing arsenal when starting a law firm, entering new markets, boosting product sales, or any other opportunity that requires a specific and personal approach.

How Can a HB Relationship Help Your Law firm?

Establishing, planning, and implementing a successful HB Relationship campaign is more complex than asking your neighbor to send a letter to his customer base with an offer from your company.

As with every other component of your marketing strategy and materials, an HB Relationship campaign must be purpose-driven and evaluated to be the best approach to secure your desired results.

For example, if your law firm caters to a broad audience and you have an irresistible offer that is going to have people running through your doors, you may want to consider a simple advertisement that will reach the most people. Alternately, if you offer a common product with a low price point – like coffee or candy – it's unlikely that a HB Relationship is worth the cost and effort involved.

So in what cases will a Host Beneficiary Relationship benefit your law firm?

1. A Start-up Company

A law firm that is just starting out has the most to gain from a HB Relationship. Faced with the standard challenges of establishing a new operation – credibility, product positioning, target market establishment, marketing strategy, etc. – a HB Relationship is an ideal way to get your law firm off the ground.

Gaining access to a time-crafted list of potential PNCs in your target market is an impressive benefit. Getting an established law firm to communicate your offer on your behalf is an almost guaranteed way to establish your own credibility.

However, start-ups often have the least to offer a 'host' company in exchange for being the 'beneficiary'. Trading PNC lists is not an option in this case. So what's in it for the 'host'?

The host is seen in the eyes of his PNCs as providing a reward or an exclusive offer for their continued support and loyalty. The host law firm earns goodwill and has an excuse to contact his database for the cost of a simple mailing.

2. Entering a New Market

An established law firm venturing into new territory is in a prime position to benefit from a HB Relationship. Whether the law firm is known or unknown in the community, tapping into a refined target list will ensure that the right people are communicated the benefits of the new law firm' offering.

In exchange, the host law firm may benefit from either the beneficiary's PNC lists in other marketplaces, or the prestige of offering PNCs an exclusive offer for a new law firm in town.

Again, this works best when the target market is highly segmented; otherwise, an advertisement would be a faster and more cost effective strategy.

3. A New Product / Service

As with new marketplaces, launching a new product or service may require tapping into a new or more segmented audience to deliver your message. An HB Relationship with the right partner will help to correctly position your offering, and deliver it to an exact audience.

The host law firm benefits by offering loyal PNCs the first opportunity to purchase or use the beneficiary law firms' product or service.

Defining Your Target Market

This is crucial in establishing an HB Relationship – just like it is crucial in every other aspect of your marketing plan. Not knowing and understanding your target market will put you on the fast track to law firm hardship, and waste time and money in the process.

You can determine your target market – or target market segment – based on the purpose or intention for seeking an HB Relationship. Are you reaching out to a new segment of your market? Are you offering a new product or service that may appeal to a specific segment of your market? Are you moving to a new market area and looking to establish yourself amongst your broader target?

Determine your audience and write your target market here:

_____

_____

_____

Selecting a Host Law firm

Once you have an idea of who your target market is, you can begin to create a list of target host law firms to approach.

Not every law firm is going to be interested or willing to engage in this marketing strategy – so doing a little bit of research and positioning your offer is well worth your while. To begin, you will want to draft a long list of all potential host law firms.

Do this by considering all law firm types that would be complementary to – but not competing with – your law firm.

Identify those law firms that offer a service or product that is connected in some way to your own. For example, my firm has an expertise in Juvenile Dependency cases. Specifically, those cases that involve parents whose children have been taken from their home by Child Protective Services (aka CPS or DCFS). Many of my colleagues don't have an expertise in this complicated area of the law, and some don't have an interest in taking on these types of cases. However, they do see clients who need this type of service. This is a perfect Host Beneficiary type of relationship. They can refer CPS cases to me (knowing I have an excellent track record) and I can refer cases to them or offer them a "referral" fee.

Pick up the yellow pages, or conduct a Google search for all law firms in your market area that fall under the categories you identified. You may also consider asking your colleagues and associates for ideas and recommendations.

When creating this list, make sure each law firm falls under these criteria:

Non-competitive. Their offer should be complementary to, but not compete with, your product or service. Make sure you consider this carefully – seemingly non-competitive offers may actually cannibalize your law firm.

Remember that your PNCs have a limited amount of money to spend, and if they begin spending money at your host's law firm, they might stop spending money at your law firm.

Same target market. If you and your host law firm are not talking to the same PNC base, then you're wasting your words on PNCs who are not likely to buy your service or product. If your host law firm has no idea who their target market is, you may also want to consider looking at other host options.

Start with your PNCs – your target market or segment of. What services do they use? What products are they interested in? Thinking about their needs will help lead you to the most effective host law firm.

A killer PNC contact list. Without this, they aren't worth approaching – but how do you know they have or maintain a PNC database? There are a couple of ways. Pay attention to the type of marketing your potential host conducts. Do they often send letters to their target market? Direct-mail flyers and other promotional materials? Or do they rely on advertising? Do they send a regular newsletter?

Positive reputation. As the beneficiary, you need to ensure that the host who is referring your law firm to their PNCs enjoys a good reputation in the community and with its clientele. Otherwise, you are being endorsed by a law firm that no one respects, which can be damaging for your reputation.

Host Law firm Ideas List

Keep track of all potential host law firms using this chart.

Law firm Name	Contact	Law firm Type
	Name: Phone:	
	Name: Phone:	
	Name: Phone:	
	Name: Phone:	
	Name: Phone:	
	Name: Phone:	
	Name: Phone:	
	Name: Phone:	

Approaching the Host Law Firm

Once you have created a list of target law firms, it is time to plan your approach. There is some strategy involved in this; you need to convince the host law firms to lend their endorsement to you in exchange for something that will benefit them.

Introduce your product or service. Present your offering to the host law firm as though you were presenting to your potential PNCs: heavy on benefits, and light on features. Assume that the host law firm has placed themselves in the shoes of their PNCs, and is evaluating whether your product or service is worthwhile for them.

Provide marketing materials and other supporting information like video testimonials and market research to establish your credibility, and your understanding of the people you are trying to reach.

Inform and excite. Provide as much information about how the HB Relationship will work, and be sincere in your efforts. Leave room for their thoughts and contributions to ensure that they buy into the process.

Get them excited about the opportunity you've placed in front of them. Use bright examples, and tell a hypothetical story about one of their PNCs benefiting from your service. Then, bring it back to the benefits that the relationship or partnership will deliver to their law firm.

Include an incentive. Be clear about the benefits the host can expect to receive. While you will not always be able to offer something tangible, do your best to offer some incentive to the host law firm.

If you are an established law firm, and if you have room in your margin, offer them a piece of the profits you receive from their PNCs. Whatever it is, make sure you articulate how this particular partnership is worth their while.

Communicate your rationale. Tell the host why you chose to approach them in particular. Do they enjoy a great reputation in the community? Are they a well-known law firm with a great sense of camaraderie? Compliment them on their law firm skills and the great relationships they have built with their PNCs and in the community.

Then, explain how your law firm can add value to theirs, and allow them to build on the existing relationships with their PNCs by offering your services.

Reassure. Communicate the benefits of the HB Relationship to the host, and reassure them that there is no risk involved for them. You are not out to take their profits, or place burden on their resources.

Remind them that you are seeking a complementary law firm relationship, one that benefits both parties.

Craft Your Message

Once you have secured your host partner, put the plan into action as quickly as possible. Offering to write the letter to their PNCs will not only give you control over the messaging of the offer, but also reduce the time investment required by the host. The process is simplified for them, and happens sooner for you.

- Just like sales letters and other marketing collateral, your HB offer letter should engage the reader and make them feel as though their needs and interests are cared for.
- The letter should position the host as a thoughtful service provider who sought out an offer specifically for the target audience.

- Your offer should be strong and slightly outrageous. Give deep discounts, or free services, exclusively to this target audience.

- Remember to acknowledge the needs and troubles of your reader, and position your product or service as the answer or solution.

- Include an incentive to act quickly. Ensure your offer is time-sensitive or of limited quantity.

Five Simple Steps to Creating an HB Relationship

In summary, here are is a five-step roadmap to creating a positive, profit-filled, HB Relationship:

- **Identify your target market.**
- **Identify target host law firms.**
- **Create a unique offer for each host law firm.**
- **Approach the host law firm.**

Draft your letter.

Points to Remember

- **Make mistakes in small batches.** If you are unsure about the accuracy of your target market – do a test run. Send a small batch of 50-100 letters to a small group of people, and measure the response.

  - Alternately, you can send three different letters to each third of your target market, and evaluate which offer is acted on the most. This is of benefit for both the host and the beneficiary law firm because the response rate of the target market is tested, as are their purchase motivations.

- **Create benefit for the host law firm.** Remember that there must be an incentive for the host law firm, or the partnership is not worth the time investment. It is important to consider this, and plan ahead before you approach the host law firm. Create a number of options for the host to choose from, whether it is using your database after the initial mailing, or sharing a piece of the profits.

- **Be honest.** If you are working with several law firms in your area on different offers, make sure each law firm knows and is comfortable with the arrangement. Ensure that each offer is distinctive and each host is benefiting from the arrangement without competing with other host law firms. This is just good law firm form.

- **Rest on the strength of your offer.** With a strong offer, your HB campaign will be on the path to success. Make it something your audience can't refuse. Your offer should not only be enticing and engaging for your audience, but should also benefit the host in reputation. Their PNCs should feel valued and appreciative toward the host for bringing your offer forward.

- **Repeat.** Once you've established one successful HB partnership, keep going! This technique is a valuable way to promote your law firm and your unique products and services, and can be repeated several times each year with several different host law firms.

Host Beneficiary Letter Template

[Headline in bold at the top of the page – strong statement or question] *[Optional sub headline to explain or answer the question/statement]*

Dear [name],

I hope this letter finds you well and enjoying [insert name or description of product or service previously purchased]. Remember, your continued satisfaction with our [product or service] is guaranteed.

I am writing because I have stumbled upon an exclusive new [product or service] that will [describe how the product or service will meet a need or solve a problem].

[Beneficiary law firm name] is a [describe law firm type] that [describe law firm function]. I recently met with the owner, and was able to secure an unbelievable rate for my existing PNCs. The

[product or service] is [describe product or service briefly]. PNCs who have already purchased have said:
[list testimonials in bullet form]

[describe limited time or quantity], we are pleased to offer you [describe unique offer here]. This is an opportunity you will not find anywhere else, and an offer that will not be available in stores.

I hope you will be able to take advantage of this amazing [product or service].

Sincerely,
[your name]
[company name]
[phone number]

HB Relationship Worksheet

Target Market:	
Potential Host 1: Name: Law firm Type:	**Unique Offer:**
Host Benefits:	**Date Contacted:**
	☐ Accepted ☐ Follow-up
Notes:	
Target Market:	
Potential Host 2: Name: Law firm Type:	**Unique Offer:**
Host Benefits:	**Date Contacted:**
	☐ Accepted ☐ Follow-up
Notes:	

A word to the wise: It is annoying for the consumer (and illegal) to send a marketing piece to someone who has not given you their permission to add their e-mail address to your mailing list. That being said, the way you can "get around this" and still use the HB relationship to grow your business, is to ask the host to "endorse" your offer and send it to his mailing list in his regular e-mail marketing campaign or newsletter.

Use caution with these e-mail lists. Otherwise, your marketing campaign and HB relationship might backfire, and cause damage to you both.

8

Use Press Releases for Instant Profit

Make Your Law firm News

The best kind of free advertising is an article in the newspaper, or a story on the radio, shining positive light on your law firm. Just like a testimonial, the printed words of a journalist are worth at least ten times more than the words in your advertising. Likewise, negative articles and reviews can cause just as much impact on your law firm – the kind of impact you don't want.

So how do you get your law firm news into the press? Better still, how do you make sure the press gets positive, accurate information about your law firm?

The simplest way to communicate with the media is through press releases. Press releases are a standard form of communication with the media, used to announce, communicate, and correct *newsworthy* information.

Press releases are not sales letters, or even newsletters. Their purpose is not to make a sale – although they may lead to sales – because they are not written for your PNC. Their purpose is to communicate news to the people that write the news, in a way that makes them take notice and care about what you have to say.

What are Effective Press Releases?

Effective press releases get your story covered. They hook editors on your angle, and encourage journalists to write about your news. They are concise, engaging, and written *with the media in mind*.

It's a good idea to sit down with your colleagues, family, and friends to test your story idea for newsworthiness. They'll be able to help you brainstorm angles and strategically plan your release.

Before you sit down to write your press release, ask yourself the following questions:

Is your story newsworthy?

If you're not used to writing press releases, spend some time thinking about this question. Of course your story is newsworthy to *you*, but why should other people care? Why does this story *matter* to the news outlet's readers? Newsworthy items are relevant, current, useful, and of importance to the community. They provide answers to the five "W's" (who, what, where, when and why).

Do you have an angle?

So your item is newsy, but what's the *angle*? Sure your law firm has had a record year for revenue, but what makes it unique? What makes your news an engaging story that is relevant to people outside your office? Did you just win a million dollar law suit? A press release should have at least one solid angle, or story idea, for the journalist. If the media have to spend time finding the story buried in your press release, you have an unlikely chance of getting covered.

Is now the right time to tell your story?

You may have a newsy story and an interesting angle, but is now the best time to tell your story? Be strategic about timing – for the benefit of your law firm, and for the likelihood of getting coverage. Strike while the iron is hot. Did the newspaper you're targeting just run a big feature on the competition? Are you waiting on other potential news that you could announce at the same time?

Is your story true?

Reporting inaccurate or exaggerated facts is bad form, and can wreak havoc on your reputation. While you wouldn't do this intentionally, check to make sure you're not embellishing the facts to create a more interesting story. Journalists are always trying to suss out the real scoop, so if you feed them garbage, they'll smell it.

Who needs to know your story?

When you craft a press release, you need to be clear on who you want to read your story. Once you know exactly who your target audience is, you can narrow your focus down to the media that reach that audience. From there, you can cater your press release to the journalists who work for those outlets.

Writing Effective Press Releases

Here are some general rules and guidelines for crafting the perfect press release. Be prepared to write a few different versions, and make substantial edits; the online press release outlets will help you do this. I use PR.com, and they have been very helpful. It takes a while to get it right. If writing is not your strongest skill, consider hiring a freelance writer to describe your news. Some online press release distribution services also offer writing services, so consider your options.

- **Craft a killer headline.** Just like advertisements, you have seconds to grab the media's attention with your headline. The headline should tell the story and answer the question *why does it matter?* Or, *why should I care?*

- **Spend time on the lead.** The lead is the first paragraph of your press release. It answers the five "W's" and provides enough detail to make the journalist or editor read on. Write a few different leads, each with a different story angle, and see which one has the most impact. If you haven't hooked them by now, consider your press release in the recycle bin.

- **Write for the newspaper.** Make your release easy to read, and easy for the journalist to work with. Occasionally, especially in communities with limited reporting resources, press releases are run with only some slight rewriting. In the best case, your release becomes the base for a feature article. Spend some time reading the publication you're targeting, and noticing the style in which it is written.

- **Notice newspaper style.** Generally, articles (and press releases) are written in an inverse pyramid format, where the most important information is as the top, and less important information follows in decreasing order of importance.

- **Use simple language.** Sentences written in simple style, with minimal description, embellishment, and flowery style are all that should appear in the release. Make sure each word has a purpose, and keep it tight. Only use the space you need to tell the story, no more.

- **Use examples to support your facts.** If you're sending a press release highlighting an achievement or accomplishment, prove it. Show the media that there are events and facts to back up your claims – cause and effect. This illustrates and tells a story, which is always more interesting and engaging than proud statements and quotes.

- **Skip industry jargon.** While industry phrases and terms may mean something to your colleagues and PNCs, they mean nothing to the media and the general public. Limit the amount of jargon you include in your release, and provide succinct explanations for uncommon terms you must use. Keep the language simple and easy to understand.

- **Use quotes sparingly.** Quotes are great ways to back up facts, add personality to your news, and include a new voice in the release. When writing quotes, keep them authentic, concise, and limited to two sources. Quotes from more than two sources in one release becomes cluttered and confusing.

- **Tell them who you are!** At the end of the release, be sure to include a short paragraph about your company that describes who you are, what you do, and a brief history.
  - **Include as much contact information as possible.** Include one or two contact names, their titles, phone numbers, email addresses, website address and cell phone numbers (if necessary). Make it as easy as possible for media to contact you.

Distribution

Media Target List

A database of local of media is a key tool for any small law firm. Whether this list is used for an ad campaign, or media relations, it is important to know the players in your local media market.

Depending on your needs – and the size of your desired reach – there are a number of ways to create this list. If you are sticking to local and regional daily media, you and your employees can easily create and maintain your database.

If you're looking to have a broader reach, there are a number of online services that provide access to PNC media lists on a one-time or subscriber basis. These services typically have the most up to date information, as well as more detailed information about media contacts that you would not find on the internet.

This list should include the name of the publication, the type of publication, the publication's frequency, a contact name, phone number and email address. In most outlets, journalists are assigned to "beats" or subjects to cover, like law firm, crime, health, and community. If you know that you are targeting the law firm section of the newspaper, make sure your release ends up in the hands of the law firm editor or reporter. Just like your marketing materials, you need to make sure your message ends up in the right hands.

Draft Media List

Outlet	Type	Name	Email	Phone
Daily News	*Newspaper*	*Jill Smith*	*jsmith@dailynews.com*	*222.555.9878*

Email Distribution

The easiest and most common form of press release distribution is by email. However, journalists are bombarded by emails and it is easy for yours to get lost in the pile. Here are some tips to make sure it gets read, and not immediately deleted.

- **Don't send attachments.** Put your news release in text format in the body of the email with simple formatting to make sure it gets read. Attachments get stuck in junk mail filters, and emails from unknown sources with attachments get deleted. To avoid this problem, use a press release outlet like PR.com or PRweb.

- **Put the headline in the subject line.** Make sure you grab the attention of your recipient with the subject line to entice them to open the email. Don't assume that everything you send will be opened. Generic subject lines get buried in inboxes, or deleted.

Distribution Services

There are also a number of reputable press release distribution networks that will distribute your release to a broad audience. Sites like prnewswire.com, PR web and PR.com allow you to send your release to state, province, country, or international market. These services also often provide writing or editing assistance, and can be valuable one-stop-shops.

Top 10 Press Release Mistakes

1. Errors in Grammar. Journalists are professional writers with a solid understanding of grammar and punctuation. Don't distract them from your news with spelling mistakes and poorly composed sentences. If writing isn't your strong suit, hire someone to write or proofread your release before you send it.

2. Too much content. The press release is intended to hook the editor, communicate the facts, and reek of newsworthiness. Once the editor or journalist is pursuing your story, you can provide them with more information and people to talk to. Stick to two pages double-spaced, max.

3. Too little content. You want to keep your release short and simple, but make sure you include all the necessary facts to support and illustrate the story. Make sure the five "W's" are answered, and all the correct contact information has been provided.

4. Sending first thing Monday morning. A journalist's inbox is the most overloaded first thing in the morning – especially on Mondays. Typically, journalists will meet with editors in the morning to review editorial assignments, then work to a mid-afternoon deadline. The best time to call and email a reporter is mid-to-late afternoon, when their deadline has passed and their inbox has been sorted through.

6. Releases that read like ads. Your press release is not an advertisement, so don't write it like one. A journalist's job is to communicate pertinent, relevant, newsworthy information to their audience, not convince them to buy your product. Avoid overused advertising catch phrases like "limited time offer" and "this won't last long!" Your job here is to communicate, not to sell.

7. Not securing permission. Make sure you have permission to mention companies other than yours, to quote sources, and to submit images of your PNCs and employees to the press. Not having permission for these items can result in your story getting pulled at the last minute.

8. Sending to multiple editors at one outlet. Pick the editor who will be most interested in your news at each target news organization, and send your release to them only. This will avoid duplication of efforts at the outlet. Often, if an editor is not interested in your news, but knows an associate editor who will be, they will give you another contact name or pass the news on directly.

9. Sending to every outlet in town. The local motorbike magazine doesn't care about news from a baby clothing business.

Make sure the media on your list are the media who would realistically cover your news. Like those specializing in legal news. Sending information that does not align with the publication's subject matter will show you haven't done your research.

10. Following up the day you send the release. It may take a few days for an editor to respond to – or even read – your release. Be patient, and wait at least a week before following up. Even then, don't assume that your release has been read or remembered. Use the opportunity to pitch the editor over the phone on your story idea, or try a new angle.

Press Release Template

For Immediate Release Date

SMART, CATCHY HEADLINE IN BOLD, CAPITALS, CENTERED AT THE TOP OF THE PAGE

Sub headline, If Some Description is Required, In Title Case Beneath Headline

City, Province OR Neighborhood, City in italics – This is the "Lead" paragraph. This paragraph should include the pertinent information – *who, what, where, and why it matters to the editor's audience.* Put yourself in the editor or journalist's shoes – why should they cover this story? Why does it matter to their readers? Is it newsworthy?

The second paragraph should elaborate on the content from the lead paragraph, and usually includes a quote from a key person (principal, president, etc.) that communicates a feeling, belief, or general view of the issue.

The third paragraph is a brief history of the event, achievement or subject of the news release. How did the company get there? What did they do to achieve this? How long have they been working to get here?

The fourth paragraph can be another quote – share another perspective or a rationale behind any controversial issues. It can also elaborate or continue from the first quote.

The fifth paragraph is about the audience – how will they benefit? What does this mean to them? What are the next steps? *The audience can include a residential community, law firm community, industry, etc.*

The sixth paragraph can highlight key points in bullet format – deadlines, dates, milestones, report highlights, key features, event details, etc.

The last paragraphs are used to explain more about the law firm – what have they done that is related to this or newsworthy? Explain more about the process – how do you achieve this? Include any other pertinent information that the audience will need to know about next steps, what to watch for etc. Include more quotes from key sources.

High resolution images of (xxx) are available upon request or – most online outlets now provide space for you to add an image.

Ends. *This shows to the reader that the news release is over.*

Media Contact *no more than two contacts, these people must be available as soon as the release is sent out*

Name, Position

Organization

Phone

Email

Press Release Sample –
New Product or Service

For Immediate Release

August 23, 2010

MOMS ON WHEELS TO DELIVER NUTRITIOUS
MEALS AT SCHOOL THIS SEPTEMBER

New lunchtime service to provide kids

with balanced snacks and meals

Cartwright, California – Attention busy moms: scratch lunches of your list. Moms on Wheels is expanding this September, providing daily lunch service for elementary school students with busy families. Parents can now subscribe to daily or weekly deliveries, and trust that convenient, healthy bag lunches are arriving at their children's classroom.

"As a mother, one of my biggest challenges is making sure my two sons go to school with a healthy and balanced lunch," says Moms on Wheels co-founder and dietician Barbara Jones. "Between grocery shopping, preparing meals, packing lunch, and making sure it winds up in their backpacks, it was taking up a lot of my time."

Moms on Wheels prepares lunches fresh every morning, then delivers to 20 elementary schools by 12:30 pm. Lunch menus vary from wraps and sandwiches, to cheese and crackers, with an assortment of seasonal vegetables, fruit and a cookie.

Moms on Wheels offers daily and weekly meal options, and caters to dietary and allergy requirements. Starting at just $3 a day, the service is affordable for every family and can be customized to a specific budget. Family rates are also available for parents with multiple children in school.

The innovative service is the brainchild of Barbara Jones and Lindsay Lee who established the meal service last year to deliver lunches once a week to local elementary schools. Jones and Lee plan to expand the service to hot items next year, when they move to an expanded kitchen facility.

To register, contact Moms on Wheels at 555.325.9872 or www.healthylunchesforkids.com. All elementary students will be bringing home an information form during the first week of school this year.

Ends.

Media Contact
Barbara Jones, Co-Founder
Moms on Wheels
555.325.9872
bjones@healthylunchesforkids.com

Press Release Sample – Accomplishment

For Immediate Release

November 12, 2009

BEND COMMUNITY LAW FIRM SWEEPS UP WITH LAW FIRM OF THE YEAR AWARD

Local law firm wins four accolades at

annual Chamber of Commerce event

Bend, Oregon – You could say that Your Law Firm truly 'cleaned up' this year; the local law firm was honored with an award in four categories at the annual Chamber of Commerce Law firm Awards. Bend Community Law Firm earned Employer of the Year Award, Story of the Year Award, Fastest Growing Law firm, and the prestigious Law firm of the Year Award.

"We are thrilled and amazed at the generous recognition we received as a company last night," said owner Jerry Owens. "These awards were earned by every member of our staff, and the terrific job they do servicing our PNCs."

Bend Community Law Firm was established by local Bend resident Jerry Owens just three years ago. Starting out with a small law firm loan from his grandfather, Gerald Carr, Owens has built the company into a thriving law firm of 25 employees, serving five communities in the region. This year, Owens hired three new attorneys specializing in Family Law, Real Estate Law and Child Dependency Law.

"It is always such a challenge to decide on a single recipient in each of the award categories, especially since there are so many reputable law firms in our community that deserve recognition," says Peter Smith, President of the Bend Chamber of Commerce. "However, we were very impressed with Mr. Owen's story, and the incredible growth of Bend Community Law Firm over the last year."

Bend Community Law Firm provides quality legal services for individuals, families, small businesses and non-profits over a wide area of Southern Oregon. They offer free consultation for many legal problems that might require an attorney.

The Chamber of Commerce Law firm Awards are held annually to recognize law firm achievement in the Bend area. For a complete list of award recipients, please contact the Chamber directly at 555.333.7659. Deadline for nominations for next year's awards is August 31, 2010.

High resolution images of the awards presentations are available upon request

Ends.

1-888-297-1616

Media Contacts:

Jerry Owens	Peter Smith
Carr's Carpet Cleaning	*Chamber of Commerce*
555.333.4337	555.333.9870
jowens@carrscarpets.com	psmith@brooksown.com

Press Release Sample – Controversy

*Note: When faced with a controversy that may affect the reputation of your law firm, consider hiring professional public relations counsel. These professionals are trained to handle challenging media relations scenarios, and can help to determine the best strategy for information disclosure.

For Immediate Release
December 15, 2009

HOLIDAY SPRUCE OFFERS FREE CHRISTMAS TREE REPLACEMENT TO ALL RESIDENTS

Trees sprayed with dangerous chemical
to be removed and replaced at no charge

Halifax, Nova Scotia – Holiday Spruce announced today that 75 per cent of the Christmas Trees for sale at their Bend Street farm have been mistreated with a chemical component that may be dangerous if repeatedly inhaled or accidentally ingested. The

Christmas tree farm is offering free removal and replacements for all families affected.

"We at Holiday Spruce are appalled by the circumstances that allowed our PNCs and families to take home mistreated Christmas trees," says Spruce Manager Tim Smith. "We sincerely apologize to the families affected by these events, and are committed to removing and replacing every single tree within the next four days."

Holiday Spruce is currently investigating the cause of the chemical mistreatment, and has closed their Bend Street farm for the season. Anyone who has purchased their holiday trees at Spruce is asked to contact their replacement line at 555.342.9020.

"We have maintained a record of each purchase made this year, and are currently in the process of contacting customers and arranging for immediate removal," says Smith. "Holiday Spruce will be purchasing trees from our associates, and delivering them to customers within the next four days."

Holiday Spruce is a seasonal tree farm on Bend Road that has been in operation for nearly 15 years. A family favorite for Christmas tree purchases, the farm offers school group tours, hot apple cider, hot dogs, and roasted chestnuts.

Ends.

Media Contact:

Tim Smith, Manager

Holiday Spruce

t. 555.342.9087

c. 555.768.3422

tsmith@holidaysprucetrees.com

9

Profit from Direct Mail

Every time you mail an existing or potential PNC a letter and ask them to respond or take action, you are running a direct-mail campaign.

Direct mail is a marketing strategy that can help you achieve a number of law firm objectives. From lead generation to PNC retention, direct mail campaigns are a highly versatile and relatively cost-effective choice for law firm promotion.

What you probably don't realize is that direct mail is one of the most targeted marketing strategies you can implement, and one of the easiest to track, measure and analyze results.

It is also one of the most personal. Instead of an advertisement, flyer, newspaper insert or catalogue, you are sending each PNC a personalized letter that is tailored to their unique needs and desires.

Getting the most out of your direct mail campaign is easy. With a laser-sharp mailing list and irresistible offer, your direct mail campaign can easily flood your law firm with qualified leads.

Let's get started!

A List of Ideal PNCs

Unless you spend time carefully crafting a mailing list of ideal PNCs, you may as well pack and up go home. The success of a direct mail campaign largely rests on the pinpoint accuracy of your mailing list.

The only people you want on your list are your potential "ideal PNCs." The people who are most likely to buy from you – often and in large volumes – and who are a delight to deal with. They are the type of people who will account for 80% of your revenue, and just 20% of your total PNC base.

You have a number of options when you are creating your mailing list:

- **Existing Client database**. This is a list of all of the people who have previously purchased from you. It is important to gather their full contact information at the time of sale so you will be able to get contact them again.

- **Existing leads database**. This is a list of all of the leads (PNC's) that have come through your door, but have not purchased from you. This may include those who responded to your last direct mail campaign, or have had a free consultation with you, but have not yet become paying clients.

- **Outsourced list**. This is a list that has been purchased from a market research firm, the government, or the post office. These lists are pulled based on demographic information and industry type – age, sex, location, income, family structure, etc.

Putting the mailing list together

Once you have determined the source(s) for your mailing list, you will have to spend some time assembling it and preparing it for your mailing.

1. Make sure all contacts are up to date. Phone old contacts to confirm their mailing address. An out-of-date list will cost you money in printing and postage.

2. Ensure all contacts are accurate to the list criteria. Take a read through your list to make sure there are no contacts that shouldn't be on the list.

3. Use a database management program to manage your mailing. This will allow you to keep a master list, and create custom lists for each mailing. Remember to save the file name as something that describes the mailing so you can easily find it.

4. **Collect e-mail addresses** – remember to always ask permission and ask if a caller or networking contact would be willing to be included on your mailing list.

Writing Effective Direct Mail Pieces

Now that you have a laser-sharp mailing list, you will want to do everything you can to target your message to the recipients on your list.

An effective direct mail piece:

- **Has a clear structure.** The piece is clearly a letter – there is an engaging headline, clear message, point form list of benefits, and postscript.

- **Features an irresistible offer.** The purchase opportunity is too good for the target audience to refuse. It includes an element of scarcity and urgency.

- **Focuses on PNC benefits.** The PNC or existing client clearly understands "what's in it for me?" The product or service is clearly positioned as something of value and a solution to a need, problem, or desire.

- **Is personal and conversational.** The letter is personally addressed, and reads as though it was composed specifically for the recipient. It is written in conversational tone, with short sentences and limited description.

- **Is short.** The letter communicates what it needs to, and closes. It does not go on for pages in length. The messages are clear, succinct, and simple.

- **Is urgent.** The piece encourages the reader to act immediately. There is a time limit or a quantity limit to the offer that requires an urgent response.

- **Includes a Postscript.** The offer or urgency is repeated after the signature at the bottom of the letter. Like a headline, everyone will read the P.S.

The Five-Step Direct Mail Campaign

1. Determine Your Target Audience

As we discussed above, you will want to ensure that you have the most accurate, targeted list possible for your direct mail campaign.

Be clear about the purpose for your direct mail campaign – this will help you decide if you want to send your letters to your entire target market, a segment of that market, existing PNCs, or potentially a referring law firm's PNCs existing clients. Then you can determine how you craft your offer, how you structure your letter, and when you choose to send it.

2. Choose what you want to say

What is the message you want to communicate to your target list? What can you offer them that will entice them to act immediately?

Create a specific offer for each direct mail campaign to ensure each time you communicate with your target list you have something new to say. Tailor this offer to each mailing list.

Decide what product or service benefits will be most compelling to your target audience, and include those benefits prominently in your letter.

3. Develop a compelling direct mail piece

You are in control of how your format your message. Are you sending a letter? A brochure and a letter? A postcard? A book? The format of your direct mail piece needs to be tailored to your target list, and reflect your product or service. A younger audience may respond to a postcard or e-mail (millennials use social platforms like Facebook, Pinterest or Twitter), but an older audience may appreciate a formalized letter.

Ensure that whatever format you choose, the piece is professionally designed, prominently includes your logo and company branding, and is professionally produced.

This piece of paper, electronic submission or social media piece, has to act as an ambassador of your company – you absolutely need it to appear impressive and professional.

4. Pick your timing

Some products and purchase decisions are best made at certain times of the year, or the month. If your law firm or service is seasonal (like a tax attorney), then there are good times and bad times to try to generate leads. Consider the best purchase windows for the people in your target marketing. When are they likely to need your service? When do they have the money to spend on your product/service? When do they spend the most money?

Anticipate these windows, and time your direct mail campaign accordingly. For example, if you ran a lawn sprinkler installation system and summer is your peak season, run a direct mail campaign mid-way through spring, and at the beginning of summer. You get the idea.

Some common time windows include:
- Holiday season (November – December)
- Seasons (Spring, Summer, Fall, Winter)
- Financial cycles (year-end, tax time)

5. Follow up

Comprehensive follow up to a direct mail campaign means two things:

1. Following up on your mailing or posting with a phone call or second mailing or posting.

Often it takes more than one mailing or posting to get a potential PNC to take action. A basic marketing fundamental is the "7 touch" concept. In other words, it takes at least "7 touches" to get a PNC to become a paying client. And then, the PNC will enter the world of becoming a paying client very tentatively until they can build trust. Be ready with different price points, so the PNC can start with a low cost item and hopefully work their way up.

If there is no response to your direct mail campaign, this can be a result of the accuracy of your mailing list, your offer, the time of the year, or the quality of the marketing material (brochure). If you are certain that your mailing list is accurate and up to date, follow up to the piece with a phone call, or send another letter, e-mail or social media posting.

Remember the "7 touch" concept.

2. Recording, measuring and analyzing your results.

It is essential that you evaluate each direct mail campaign based on your time and financial investment and your rate of response. How else will you be able to tell if it was a successful or effective strategy?

For each campaign, record and analyze the following information:

- Number of letters or e-mails sent, or social media postings made
- Number of responses as a percentage
- Number of sales directly resulting from the campaign
- Number of inquiries
- Total value of sales directly resulting from the campaign

Based on this information, determine if the campaign was successful (did it make you money? Or, money may not be your only measurement. Perhaps it's PNC's?). Consider making some changes to your list, your offer, or the piece itself, and try again.

10

Organize Your Office for Success

Have you ever tried to cook a fancy gourmet dinner in a messy kitchen?

It starts out okay. I have all the ingredients I need; it just takes me a little longer to find them as I go. I have to find and clear some counter space, then wipe the crumbs off of it and grab a knife.

Some pots are clean, so I use them first. But then I need the double boiler, and it's still crusted with last night's meal, so I have to wash it. While I'm washing the pot, the garlic and onion that I'm sautéing starts to burn, so I have to run over and rescue it.

Pretty soon, I'm running around like crazy, trying to rescue each item I cook because I'm busy preparing what I need for the next dish. It should be no surprise that the meal was a disaster.

Your place of work is just like your kitchen. It needs to be clean, well-organized, and ready to function. Your tools need to be prepared and at the ready in order to support the tasks you and your staff need to complete.

A well set-up office – with all the necessary tools – will save you time and the expense of redundancy. This is the first key to an effective and successful law firm operation.

Create an Office for Profitability

Most people understand the relationship between time management and profitability. Effective time management increases productivity; more work can be completed in less time, with less distraction and waste.

Office organization also affects profitability and productivity. A tidy and well-structured office is not only a more pleasant place to work, but it also reduces the time anyone might spend looking for items and digging through loose paperwork.

A well-organized office also encourages better internal communication. There are clear areas of the law firm that are designated for sales news, target tracking, and project planning. This fosters team building and collaborative work ethic.

Getting Started: Workspace Audit

The best place to start is by taking an honest inventory of the current state of your office or working environment. With that information, you can determine what areas need to be improved, streamlined, or de-cluttered. Spend some time taking a look around your office and note the following:

- Is there a location where internal company information is displayed?
- What is the distance between your office and the printer or photocopier?
- How much lose paper is found around your office?
- What is hung up on the walls? Are posters and important papers hung on the walls with visible tape? Or are they neatly organized and hung with tape that is invisibly placed on the corners?
- Do your staff members have organization systems for their own desks?
- What can be found on your desk?
- How many files are used on a daily or weekly basis?
- Where are old or outdated files kept?

Organize Your Desk

Presumably, your desk is where you spend the most time in your office. It is where you are expected to be the most productive.

To get all your important tasks completed.

Simply put, you will be more productive and effective if your workspace is clean and organized. Spend some time each day tidying and organizing your workspace – ideally when you are planning your work or your schedule for the following day. Think of yourself as a new client. What kind of impression do you have if your attorney's office is a mess wih loose papers everywhere. If you are like most people, you wll have the impression of "disorganization". This is not a good impression from an attorney who is responsible for your very important papers – is his/her mind as cluttered as his/her office?

Here are some other ways you can keep your immediate workspace in the most productive form possible:

Phone. Put your phone on the left side of the desk if you are right handed and on the right side of the desk if you are left handed. Keep a notebook by the phone to record messages and conversation notes. Also record phone messages here, and delete them from your system.

Personal Items. Keep personal items out of your immediate line of sight. Pictures can be distracting, and points for daydreaming. An alternative way of thinking about personal items, is to encourage your associates to display a few items of a personal nature. This humanizes a person that has much more education and expertise than the average client, therefore leveling the playing field and making the attorney/client relationship much more trusting and productive.

Organizer. Keep your Daytimer or PDA easily accessible on your desk. Use this as your main system for notes, tasks, follow-up, and brainstorming. Keep the rest of your desk clear.

Files. Only keep the files you need on your desk or within arm's reach. Store any files you don't use daily or weekly in a filing cabinet further away.

Inbox and action items. Sort items in your inbox into an easily accessible file sorter or a stack of paper trays. Separate paper into the following categories: to-do, to-review, waiting response, on-hold, to file.

Organize Your Office

Take the information you gathered in your workplace audit and identify opportunities for improvement. Can the office benefit from a better layout? A paper management system? More clearly defined areas? A new filing system?

The answer will depend on the unique needs of your law firm, and take into account how you and your staff & associates use the space. Here are some suggestions and guidelines for improving the organization of your office or law firm:

Establish Clear Areas

Divide your law firm into areas of productivity, and locate all related materials and equipment in each area.

Here are some sample areas you may wish to consider:

- Printing and photocopying – for example, if your work space allows, it is my recommendation that this is a function that's relegated to a separate room, with a closed door, or out of the line of sight of PNCs.
- Office supplies – again – see my recommendation above.
- Financial paperwork and accounting – I actually have this function on a totally separate floor. Not all law firms have this luxury – but you get the idea.
- Team gathering
- Kitchen or food-related preparation – smells can be really "off-putting" to some people. Please encourage staff and associates to eat and/or prepare food in a separate lunchroom or offsite. Nothing is so unprofessional as a receptionist or associate eating in their workspace.
- Reception

Create a Central Location for Information

Many people – including your staff and associates – learn and interpret information that is visual better than any other means of communication. A central location in your office for staff to go for company information and updates is an essential tool for team building and internal communications.

Every office needs:

Whiteboard

Place a whiteboard in an easily accessed place – your staff communication center or the main conference room. This whiteboard is for brainstorming, project planning, marketing planning, or any other use that may be required.

This is a great tool for team meetings, PNC meetings, and management meetings. For example, the attorney handling a PNC consult can diagram information and work through issues on the spot. Ideally, the white board can be easily "closed" or "covered" so it is not a distraction to future meetings that are scheduled for that space.

Sales Board

Create a customized sales board for your law firm. This should not be in an area that can be seen by PNCs or existing clients. Take a whiteboard, and some thin black tape, and create a chart or diagram that records regular sales statistics and targets.

Compare your targets based on weekly, quarterly, and yearly results/goals. For example, you can compare actual PNC consultations for the same time period the previous year.

12-Month Marketing Planner

Chart your marketing plan on a large calendar and post it in a central area. This is a clear reminder of the big picture, and each of the books, promotions, brochures or direct mail pieces you have planned over the course of the year.

Remember to write in dry-erase marker so you can easily make changes. Consider color-coding your promotions or projects for easy visibility.

Manage Paper + Filing

System	Steps
Create a master filing system and color code it	Group vendor files (accounts payable) and assign a color Group PNC files (accounts receivable) and assign a color Group project or product files and assign a color
Sort each filing category by date or alphabetically by name	Sort vendor or supplier files by name Sort PNC files by PNC number or name Sort project files by project number or name
Create a binder (or electronic database) of master lists for regularly accessed information	Office passwords Financial accounts Goals Birthdays Vendor contact information

Use a bound notebook Or electronic database	Keep track of phone calls and messages Put the date on each page Eliminate loose notepaper
Get rid of magazines and other reading material	Throw away industry magazines and newspapers Keep relevant articles of interest Sort them into files, if necessary
Keep tax-related documents in one spot	File all receipts, donations and other tax related information in the same filing cabinet Make copies of documents you need to file in more than one spot
Create a law firm care management system	Throw away old law firm cards Enter the information in a data management program, then throw away the cards

11

So What Do You Do From Here?

Take action! If you are already an accomplished law firm owner burning in excess of $200,000 per year, use this book as direction to enhance the speed of your law firm success. If you are not as accomplished as you would like to be, just remember: The amazing thing about the game of law firm marketing and sales is that when you put proven processes to work and continue to follow them, and abundance of success will follow. The biggest mistake is to start a process and then fall back into your old habits after a short time. The thing to do is:

A) Read this book

B) Implement the strategies in this book – don't get overwhelmed – implement one strategy at a time. Do it well & measure the results. Did it work as you had planned? If not, why not?

C) Call Vince for periodic review and modification to your Marketing & Sales strategies.

Concentrate on strategies to learn and the turn will follow! If you are serious about taking the next step then go to work on yourself, study other law firm's successes, understand marketing strategies and become a sponge for new material. The amazing thing about the game of law firm marketing and sales is that when you put proven processes to work and continue to follow them, an abundance of success will follow. The biggest mistake is to start a process and then fall back into your old habits after a short time.

Above all, get the knowledge you need to before you step onto the field. Think about it, if you were going to challenge Michael Jordan to a game of basketball for money, wouldn't it make sense to learn the game and practice before you stepped onto the court? It is amazing to me how many new small and medium law firms start the game of lawyering against seasoned professionals, the competition, without the first developing the necessary knowledge to be successful. Then they feel and blame the market, the economy, their location, the PNCs, etc.

If you have a law firm and have not yet managed to create wealth and systems that allow you to take time off, bill retirement accounts or pay for your children's college, then learn and master the steps outlined in my book. I am a huge advocate of education and mentorships. Get the right information, find someone that knows how to walk you through them, and watch your quality of life take new shape.

To learn how to avoid the three key mistakes all small and medium law firms make, visit www.LegalMarketingAndSalesCoach.com.